MEDITERRANEAN DIET COOKBOOK FOR BEGINNERS

1500 Days of Quick & Simple Recipes to Build Healthy Habits and 60-Day Meal Plan to Lose Weight

Table of Contents

What is Mediterranean Diet?

One of the favorite diets all over the world is the Mediterranean diet. It is a plant-based macrobiotic diet that was created in the Mediterranean regions of Europe. This way of eating is the secret to the long healthy life of indigenous people. The Mediterranean diet doesn't include complicated ingredients. As usual, it is various fruits and vegetables. Fatty and processed food are not recommended during the diet. There is a Mediterranean pyramid that helps people all over the world easily follow the diet. This pyramid was created by Harvard school around 25 years ago. The main place in this pyramid takes whole grains, nuts, legumes, seeds, and beans, and the fewest is for dairy products, meats, and sweets.

The Mediterranean diet has many benefits but the biggest is its feature to reduce and stop developing heart diseases. Nevertheless, the diet fights well with different inflammations and can help in weight loss. However, the Diet needs to be followed long time and constantly; like that, you will get the desirable result.

The Mediterranean diet is perfect for people with 2 types of diabetes. As usual, physicians recommend it as a healthy meal plan. Besides this, if you don't have any health problems, you can follow them to maintain your body and strengthen it.

As with every diet, the Mediterranean diet has not only advantages. The bad side of the diet is that it doesn't have a special guide and food list. The consumption of daily calories is also unclear – there is no certain number. As the ingredients for the diet are grown in the Mediterranean region, some of them it's hard to find in the States. Some ingredients can be pricy and you can find them only in shops with organic food.

All the disadvantages are easy to avoid if you are ready to follow the diet seriously. Constantly following the diet will bring you stunning results. If you try this diet once, you will make it your lifestyle.

What to Eat and Avoid on Mediterranean Diet

Grain Products

Whole grains are the fundament of the Mediterranean diet. They have all vital minerals for our body such as zinc, magnesium, and iron; the whole grains are rich in fiber, antioxidants, and B vitamins. In addition, these products help to fight and avoid diabetes problems and high blood pressure. Also, they help to lower the stroke risk.

WHAT TO EAT	EAT OCCASIONALLY	WHAT TO AVOID
− Whole-grain:	− Whole-grain pasta	− White rice
− oatmeal	− Whole-grain noodles	− Regular pasta
− popcorn	− Pita bread	− White bread
− millet	− Brown rice	− Refined grains (white flour)
− quinoa		
− brown rice		
− whole rye		
− wild rice		
− wheat berry		
− bulgur		
− buckwheat		
− freekeh		
− barley		
− sorghum		

Meat and Poultry

Meat and poultry are not so important while dieting. The consumption of these products should be limited. They can be served as a compliment to your main dishes which in most should be vegetables.

WHAT TO EAT	EAT OCCASIONALLY	WHAT TO AVOID
− Skinless chicken breast	− Lean cuts of red meat (pork, beef, veal, lamb)	− Cured and processed meat:
− Skinless chicken thighs		− Bacon
− Skinless chicken wings		− Salami
− Skinless drumsticks		− Sausages
− Chicken fillet		− Pork belly

Fish and Seafood

It is recommended to serve the fish and seafood dishes at least 2-3 times per week. They are the main source of Omega-3 and proteins.

WHAT TO EAT	WHAT TO AVOID
− Salmon	− High-sodium/salted canned fish and seafood
− Herring	
− Tuna	
− Mackerel	
− Sardines	
− Cod	
− Clams	
− Lobsters	

Vegetables

The basis of nutrition while dieting is vegetables. They are rich in minerals, vitamins, and microelements. You can consume as many vegetables as you want. The best ways to cook them are grilling or steaming. It is not recommended to fry vegetables as a high amount of oil is harmful.

WHAT TO EAT	WHAT TO AVOID
– All fresh vegetables and greens	– Regular canned vegetables

Fruits and Berries

Fruits and berries are the perfect addition to your salads and desserts. At the same time, you can eat them as snacks during the day. They have the same value as vegetables and are not less rich in vitamins and microelements.

WHAT TO EAT	WHAT TO AVOID
– All fruits and berries (pineapple, apple, mango, pears, strawberries, raspberries, dates, apricots, etc.)	– Sugar-added canned fruits – Sugar-added dried fruits

Dairy Products

Dairy products serve as a source of calcium and D vitamin while dieting. The best choice for the Mediterranean diet is plain yogurt and different types of cheese.

WHAT TO EAT	EAT OCCASIONALLY	WHAT TO AVOID
– Burrata – Feta – Mozzarella – Parmigiano-Reggiano (Parmesan) – Cream cheese – Plain Yogurt – Greek Yogurt – Free-range eggs	– Milk	– Highly-processed cheese

Nuts, Seeds, and Legumes

They are the richest in plant proteins and fiber. This type of food should be included in your daily diet. Moreover, nuts, seeds, and legumes cause fewer heart problems in comparison with animal protein.

This food is rich in proteins and dietary fiber. It is the main source of useful microelements if you are vegetarian/vegan, or follow religious fasting. Nuts, seeds, and legumes should be included in your diet daily. The protein which you get from nuts, seeds, and legumes causes fewer heart diseases in comparison with animal proteins.

WHAT TO EAT
– All types of seeds – All types of nuts – All types of legumes

Fats and Oils

Oil helps our body to avoid blood clots. The oil is one of the most popular dressings for the Mediterranean diet. You can also add it to the main dishes. You should avoid animal fats as they are harmful to the body.

WHAT TO EAT	ENJOY OCCASIONALLY	WHAT TO AVOID
− Olive oil − Avocado oil − Grape seeds oil	− Canola oil − Ghee (clarifies butter)	− Animal fats − Hydrogenated oils (palm oil, palm kernel oil)

Sweets

It is not recommended to eat fruits while dieting. The best source of glucose for the Mediterranean diet still stays fruits and vegetables; sweet and sparkling drinks can be substituted with fresh juices.

WHAT TO EAT	ENJOY OCCASIONALLY	WHAT TO AVOID
− Fruit/berries sorbets − Fruit ice − Sugar-free fruit jelly − Cinnamon	− Baked fruits − Honey	− Candies − Sweet baked goods/desserts − Syrup-sweetened drinks (soda, artificial juices)

Alcohol and Caffeine

You can drink coffee with caffeine while dieting; however, do it in moderation. If we talk about alcohol, it is not strictly forbidden. Men can allow one glass of wine per day, and for women, this limit is – a half glass of wine.

ENJOY OCCASIONALLY	WHAT TO AVOID
− Wine	− tequila − vodka − hard liquors

Top 10 Tips for Mediterranean Diet

1.   Sport activities are important.

Mediterranean diet does all to help you lose weight; however, only sport can keep you fit and help you feel young not only inside. Diversify your day by jogging, running, or attending the gym.

2.   All is step-by-step.

Don't hurry up with the diet and add new healthy food gradually. It will help you to follow the diet constantly. Moreover, it will help to less the stress for your body and stay full during the day.

3.   Meal list for the day.

As you know, the Mediterranean diet doesn't have a strict caloric following. To protect yourself from overeating make a meal list for the day. You can easily do using your phone or notebook.

4.   Antioxidants are important.

They help our body to fight free radicals. The best berries for your Mediterranean diet are raspberries and blueberries.

5.   Make taste better.

As you avoid eating much salt, add spices to your diet. Such spices as chili pepper, cayenne pepper, garlic, onion, and basil will make your meal much better.

6.   Raw food is useful.

All eat all fruits and some vegetables fresh. Doing this, you will get more benefits from them.

7.   Eat healthy proteins.

As you know nuts, seeds, and legumes are the best source of plant protein. However, if you can't exclude meat from your diet, eat lean types of meat not more than 2 times per week.

8.   Consume with the mind.

If you can't give up alcohol while dieting, always chooses the right wine with a "USDA organic label". Such wine is always done from organic grapes.

9.   Smart dairy.

Not all dairy is good for the Mediterranean diet. It is recommended to consume fermented dairies such as cheese and cream cheese. Eat plain yogurt in moderation and avoid full-fat milk.

10.   No junk food.

Prepare vegetables, fruits, nuts, or seeds for your daily snack. It will help you to avoid eating junk food during the day.

BREAKFAST RECIPES

Breakfast Recipes

Dill Eggs

Yield: 2 servings | **Prep time:** 5 minutes
Cook time: 5 minutes

Ingredients:

- 1 tomato, chopped
- 1 teaspoon canola oil
- 1 cup fresh dill, chopped
- 3 eggs, beaten
- 1 oz Feta cheese, crumbled

Directions:

1. Heat canola oil in the pan.
2. Then add chopped tomatoes and dill. Cook the ingredients for 2 minutes.
3. After this, add eggs and stir the mixture well.
4. Cook the meal for 2 minutes more, add feta cheese, and stir well. Cook the meal for 1 minute more.

per serving: 167 calories, 10.5g protein, 4.2g carbohydrates, 12.2g fat, 1.4g fiber, 258mg cholesterol, 269mg sodium, 336mg potassium.

Quinoa Bowl

Yield: 6 servings | **Prep time:** 10 minutes
Cook time: 7 minutes

Ingredients:

- ¼ cup plain yogurt
- 12 eggs
- ¼ teaspoon ground black pepper
- ½ teaspoon salt
- 1 tablespoon canola oil
- 1 cup Roma tomatoes, chopped
- 1 cup quinoa, cooked
- 1 cup fresh parsley, chopped
- 1 red onion, sliced

Directions:

1. Boil the eggs in the water for 7 minutes. Then cool them in cold water and peel.
2. Chop the eggs roughly and put them in the salad bowl.
3. Add plain yogurt, ground black pepper, salt, canola oil, tomatoes, quinoa, parsley, and red onion.
4. Shake the mixture well.

per serving: 283 calories, 15.2g protein, 22.6g carbohydrates, 11g fat, 2.9g fiber, 328mg cholesterol, 325mg sodium, 409mg potassium.

Walnut Oats

Yield: 2 servings | **Prep time:** 5 minutes
Cook time: 0 minutes

Ingredients:

- 1 oz walnuts, chopped
- ¼ cup oats
- ½ cup Greek yogurt
- 1 date, chopped

Directions:

1. Mix up all ingredients together and leave for 5 minutes.
2. Then transfer the meal to the serving bowls.

per serving: 198 calories, 6.5g protein, 16.4g carbohydrates, 11.6g fat, 2.7g fiber, 4mg cholesterol, 44mg sodium, 268mg potassium.

Feta Frittata

Yield: 6 servings | **Prep time:** 10 minutes
Cook time: 20 minutes

Ingredients:

- ¼ cup kalamata olives, pitted and chopped
- 8 eggs, beaten
- 2 cups fresh parsley, chopped
- 1 tablespoon canola oil
- ½ teaspoon chili flakes
- 2 oz Feta, crumbled
- ¼ cup plain yogurt

Directions:

1. Brush the pan with olive oil.
2. After this, in the mixing bowl, mix up all remaining ingredients and pour the mixture into the pan.
3. Bake the frittata for 20 minutes at 355F.

per serving: 145 calories, 9.6g protein, 2.3g carbohydrates, 10.9g fat, 0.4g fiber, 227mg cholesterol, 252mg sodium, 165mg potassium.

Sweet Paprika Eggs

Yield: 6 servings | **Prep time:** 10 minutes
Cook time: 20 minutes

Ingredients:

- 2 green sweet peppers, chopped
- 3 tablespoons olive oil
- 1 yellow onion, chopped
- 1 teaspoon sweet paprika
- 6 tomatoes, chopped
- 6 eggs
- ¼ cup fresh dill, chopped

Directions:

1. Heat a pan with the oil over medium heat, add all ingredients except eggs, and roast them for 5 minutes.
2. Stir the vegetables well and crack the eggs.
3. Transfer the pan with eggs to the preheated 360F oven and bake them for 15 minutes.

per serving: 169 calories, 7.1g protein, 10g carbohydrates, 11.8g fat, 2.6g fiber, 164mg cholesterol, 71mg sodium, 174mg potassium.

Shiitake Mushrooms Casserole

Yield: 4 servings | **Prep time:** 10 minutes
Cook time: 60 minutes

Ingredients:

- 2 eggs, beaten
- 5 oz Shiitake mushrooms, sliced
- 2 shallots, chopped
- 1 teaspoon marjoram, dried
- ½ cup artichoke hearts, chopped
- 3 oz Parmesan cheese, shredded
- ½ cup Greek yogurt

Directions:

1. Mix up all ingredients in the casserole mold and cover it with foil.
2. Bake the casserole for 60 minutes at 355F.

per serving: 175 calories, 11.5g protein, 6.2g carbohydrates, 9.5g fat, 1.3g fiber, 106mg cholesterol, 204mg sodium, 272mg potassium.

Cinnamon Pancakes

Yield: 2 servings | **Prep time:** 10 minutes
Cook time: 5 minutes

Ingredients:

- 6 ounces sour cream
- ½ cup whole-grain flour
- 1 egg, beaten
- 1 teaspoon ground cinnamon
- 1 teaspoon baking powder

Directions:

1. Heat a non-stick skillet well.
2. Meanwhile, mix up all ingredients together.
3. Pour the mixture into the skillet in the shape of the pancakes.
4. Cook them for 1 minute per side.

per serving: 210 calories, 10.7g protein, 29.4g carbohydrates, 3.9g fat, 3.7g fiber, 87mg cholesterol, 94mg sodium, 606mg potassium.

Chives Galettes

Yield: 4 servings | **Prep time:** 10 minutes
Cook time: 30 minutes

Ingredients:

- 4 oz chives, chopped
- ¼ cup bell pepper, chopped
- ½ teaspoon salt
- 1 teaspoon chili powder
- 2 tablespoons olive oil
- 1 teaspoon dried parsley
- 6 eggs, beaten
- 2 tablespoons plain yogurt

Directions:

1. Mix up chives, bell pepper, salt, and chili powder in the pan.
2. Add olive oil and dried parsley. Saute the ingredients for 5 minutes.
3. Then pour the beaten eggs into the square baking mold.
4. Add sauteed chives mixture and plain yogurt. Flatten the mixture well and bake in the preheated to 360F oven for 20 minutes.
5. Cut the meal into galettes.

per serving: 187 calories, 10.1g protein, 2.4g carbohydrates, 13.2g fat, 0.3g fiber, 246mg cholesterol, 390mg sodium, 140mg potassium.

Mozzarella Frittata

Yield: 12 servings | **Prep time:** 10 minutes
Cook time: 25 minutes

Ingredients:

- 3 garlic cloves, minced
- 1 tablespoon canola oil
- 1 cup fresh spinach, chopped
- 8 eggs, beaten
- 1 teaspoon ground black pepper
- 1 cup mozzarella cheese, shredded

Directions:

1. Pour canola oil into the pan and heat it.
2. Mix up eggs with ground black pepper, spinach, and garlic cloves.
3. Pour the mixture into the hot pan.
4. Top the egg mixture with Mozzarella and transfer in the preheated to 360F oven.
5. Bake the frittata for 20 minutes.

per serving: 59 calories, 4.3g protein, 0.7g carbohydrates, 4.8g fat, 0.1g fiber, 110mg cholesterol, 56mg sodium, 51mg potassium.

Artichoke Eggs

Yield: 4 servings | **Prep time:** 5 minutes
Cook time: 10 minutes

Ingredients:

- 4 eggs, beaten
- 1 tomato, chopped
- ½ cup artichoke hearts, chopped
- 4 oz Feta cheese, crumbled
- 1 tablespoon avocado oil

Directions:

1. Mix up eggs, chopped artichokes, Feta cheese, and tomato.
2. Then brush the baking mold with avocado oil and pour the mixture inside.
3. Bake the eggs for 10 minutes at 365F.

per serving: 242 calories, 14.9g protein, 3.2g carbohydrates, 17g fat, 1.1g fiber, 193mg cholesterol, 175mg sodium, 169mg potassium.

Tomato Frittata

Yield: 4 servings | **Prep time:** 10 minutes
Cook time: 15 minutes

Ingredients:

- 1 cup red bell pepper, chopped
- 1 tablespoon canola oil
- 1 tomato, sliced
- 4 eggs, beaten
- ¼ teaspoon ground paprika
- ¼ teaspoon salt

Directions:

1. Brush the baking pan with canola oil.
2. Then add all remaining ingredients, mix gently, and transfer to the preheated 365F oven.
3. Cook the frittata for 15 minutes.

per serving: 125 calories, 6.2g protein, 3.3g carbohydrates, 8g fat, 0.6g fiber, 164mg cholesterol, 210mg sodium, 153mg potassium.

Cod Eggs

Yield: 4 servings | **Prep time:** 5 minutes
Cook time: 20 minutes

Ingredients:

- 1 cup sweet potato, chopped, cooked
- 1 tablespoon avocado oil
- 10 oz cod fillet, chopped
- ¼ cup broccoli, chopped
- 4 eggs, beaten

Directions:

1. Mash the sweet potato and mix it with chopped cod, and broccoli.
2. Then heat avocado oil in the pan.
3. Add mashed sweet potato mixture and cook it for 10 minutes. Stir from time to time.
4. After this, add eggs, and whisk the mixture gently.
5. Close the lid and cook it for 10 minutes more.

per serving: 210 calories, 19.5g protein, 11.2g carbohydrates, 7.3g fat, 2g fiber, 195mg cholesterol, 113mg sodium, 599mg potassium.

Cheese Tortillas

Yield: 4 serving | **Prep time:** 5 minutes
Cook time: 10 minutes

Ingredients:

- 4 eggs, beaten
- 1 teaspoon olive oil
- 6 oz chicken fillet, minced
- 3 oz goat cheese, crumbled
- 4 lettuce leaves
- 4 corn tortillas

Directions:

1. Heat a pan with the oil over medium heat, add eggs, cheese, and minced chicken, stir gently, and cook until eggs thicken.
2. Then top the tortillas with lettuce leaves.
3. Add the cooked egg mixture and wrap the tortillas.

per serving: 191 calories, 12.2g protein, 11.8g carbohydrates, 9.6g fat, 1.7g fiber, 179mg cholesterol, 139mg sodium, 157mg potassium.

Lentil Bowl

Yield: 4 servings | **Prep time:** 10 minutes
Cook time: 10 minutes

Ingredients:

- 2 cups lettuce, chopped
- ½ teaspoon ginger powder
- 1 white onion, diced
- ½ teaspoon salt
- ½ teaspoon white pepper
- 1 teaspoon ground paprika
- 3 cups red lentils, boiled
- 1 tablespoon olive oil

Directions:

1. Heat olive oil in the pan.
2. Add onion, ginger, dill, salt, white pepper, and ground paprika, and stir the ingredients well.
3. Cook them for 5 minutes.
4. Then add lentils, stir well, and cook the meal for 5

minutes more.

per serving: 487 calories, 22.8g protein, 74.8g carbohydrates, 10.1g fat, 21.9g fiber, 0mg cholesterol, 272mg sodium, 1164mg potassium.

Eggs and Olives

Yield: 4 servings | **Prep time:** 5 minutes
Cook time: 10 minutes

Ingredients:

- 4 eggs
- 1 tablespoon olive oil
- 4 green olives, pitted, sliced
- 1 cherry tomato, sliced
- ¼ teaspoon ground black pepper

Directions:

1. Heat olive oil in the pan.
2. Then crack the eggs in it.
3. Sprinkle the eggs with green olives, sliced tomato, and ground black pepper.
4. Close the lid and cook the meal for 7 minutes over medium-low heat.

per serving: 110 calories, 5.7g protein, 2.1g carbohydrates, 8.4g fat, 0.3g fiber, 164mg cholesterol, 248mg sodium, 89mg potassium.

Onion Beans

Yield: 3 servings | **Prep time:** 10 minutes
Cook time: 10 minutes

Ingredients:

- 1 ½ tablespoon olive oil
- 1 tomato, chopped
- 1 white onion, minced
- 1 cup white beans, boiled
- ½ teaspoon salt
- ½ teaspoon chili powder

Directions:

1. Heat olive oil in the pan.
2. Add chopped tomato, salt, and chili powder.
3. Cook the mixture for 3 minutes.
4. Then add onion and white beans. Stir the ingredients well and cook over medium-low heat for 7 minutes.

per serving: 273 calories, 14.1g protein, 39g carbohydrates, 7.8g fat, 9.7g fiber, 0mg cholesterol, 400mg sodium, 895mg potassium.

Quinoa with Pecans

Yield: 4 servings | **Prep time:** 10 minutes
Cook time: 0 minutes

Ingredients:

- 2 cups coconut milk, warm
- 1 teaspoon vanilla extract
- ¼ 4 pecans, chopped
- 1 ½ cup quinoa, cooked
- 2 tablespoons honey
- 2 dates, dried, pitted, and chopped

Directions:

1. Mix all ingredients in the big saucepan and close the lid.
2. Leave the meal for 10 minutes in a warm place.
3. Then stir it gently one more time and transfer it into the serving bowls.

per serving: 346 calories, 10.9g protein, 58.1g carbohydrates, 8.1g fat, 5.6g fiber, 0mg cholesterol, 74mg sodium, 437mg potassium.

Fennel Salad with Dill

Yield: 4 servings | **Prep time:** 10 minutes
Cook time: 0 minutes

Ingredients:

- 2 garlic cloves, diced
- 2 tablespoons olive oil
- 1 tablespoon lemon juice
- ¼ cup fresh dill, chopped
- ½ cup black olives, sliced
- 2 cups lettuce, chopped
- 1 fennel bulb, chopped

Directions:

1. Mix up all ingredients in the salad bowl.
2. Shake the salad well.

per serving: 101 calories, 1.3g protein, 7g carbohydrates, 9g fat, 2.7g fiber, 0mg cholesterol, 182mg sodium, 318mg potassium.

Yogurt Muffins

Yield: 4 servings | **Prep time:** 10 minutes
Cook time: 8 minutes

Ingredients:

- 1 tomato, chopped
- 4 eggs, beaten
- ¼ cup plain yogurt
- 1 teaspoon dried oregano
- 1 teaspoon avocado oil
- ¼ cup Cheddar cheese, shredded

Directions:

1. Mix up all ingredients in the bowl.
2. Pour the liquid into the muffin molds and bake them in the preheated to 365F oven for 8 minutes.

per serving: 102 calories, 7.8g protein, 3.6g carbohydrates, 6.4g fat, 0.2g fiber, 166mg cholesterol, 84mg sodium, 145mg potassium.

Banana and Raspberry Bowl

Yield: 4 servings | **Prep time:** 10 minutes
Cook time: 5 minutes

Ingredients:

- 1 cup bananas, chopped
- 2 cups raspberries
- 1 tablespoon almond flakes
- 4 tablespoons Greek yogurt

Directions:

1. In the serving bowls, mix up bananas and raspberries. Shake the ingredients gently and top with almond flakes and Greek yogurt.

per serving: 73 calories, 2.5g protein, 15g carbohydrates, 0.9g fat, 2.5g fiber, 1mg cholesterol, 7mg sodium, 244mg potassium.

Strawberry Bars

Yield: 12 servings | **Prep time:** 35 minutes
Cook time: 5 minutes

Ingredients:

- ½ cup dates, chopped
- 1 teaspoon vanilla extract
- 2 tablespoons Erythritol
- 1 cup rolled oats
- ¾ cup strawberries, dried
- ¼ cup of canola oil
- 1 cup almonds, chopped

Directions:

1. Melt the canola oil with Erythritol.
2. Then add vanilla extract, dates, rolled oats, strawberries, and almonds. Stir the mixture until homogenous.
3. After this, transfer the mixture to the lined baking tray and flatten it well.
4. Leave the mixture in the fridge for 30 minutes or until the meal is solid.
5. Then cut it into the bars.

per serving: 177 calories, 6.8g protein, 15.4g carbohydrates, 8.7g fat, 2.5g fiber, 0mg cholesterol, 1mg sodium, 145mg potassium.

Goat Cheese Sandwich

Yield: 2 servings | **Prep time:** 10 minutes
Cook time: 5 minutes

Ingredients:

- 4 lettuce leaves
- 2 oz Goat cheese, crumbled
- 1 egg, beaten
- ½ teaspoon avocado oil
- ¼ teaspoon chili powder
- ¼ teaspoon ground turmeric
- ¼ teaspoon salt
- 1 tomato, sliced

Directions:

1. Heat the avocado oil in the pan.
2. Then mix up egg, chili powder, salt, and ground turmeric.
3. Pour the egg mixture into the pan and cook it for 1.5 minutes per side.
4. Then cut the egg pancake into halves and put on 2 lettuce leaves.
5. Add goat cheese and tomato.
6. Top the tomato with the remaining lettuce.

per serving: 133 calories, 7.3g protein, 3.2g carbohydrates, 7.3g fat, 0.6g fiber, 107mg cholesterol, 643mg sodium, 148mg potassium.

Mozzarella Bowl

Yield: 4 servings | **Prep time:** 10 minutes
Cook time: 20 minutes

Ingredients:

- 1 cup sweet potatoes, chopped
- ½ red onion, diced
- 3 ounces pancetta, chopped
- 1 ½ tablespoon olive oil
- ¼ cup mozzarella, shredded
- 1 tablespoon fresh parsley, chopped
- 1 cup water, for cooking

Directions:

1. Mix up sweet potato and water and boil the mixture for 15 minutes or until the sweet potato is soft.
2. Then drain the water and transfer the sweet potato to the serving bowls.
3. Roast pancetta with olive oil and onion over medium heat for 5 minutes. Stir it from time to time.
4. Then add the ingredients to the sweet potato bowls.
5. Top the meal with parsley and Mozzarella.

per serving: 208 calories, 9g protein, 10.9g carbohydrates, 14.4g fat, 1.6g fiber, 24mg cholesterol, 507mg sodium, 429mg potassium

Blackberry Eggs

Yield: 4 servings | **Prep time:** 10 minutes
Cook time: 5 minutes

Ingredients:

- 3 eggs, beaten
- ½ teaspoon avocado oil
- 1 teaspoon ground cinnamon
- 2 oz cottage cheese
- 1 cup blackberries

Directions:

1. Mix up eggs with ground cinnamon, and cottage cheese.
2. Heat olive oil in the skillet and pour the egg mixture inside.
3. Cook it for 2 minutes.
4. Then flip the egg cake to another side and cook for 1 minute more.
5. Cut the egg pancake into 4 servings and top with blueberries.

per serving: 89 calories, 6.4g protein, 6.6g carbohydrates, 4.4g fat, 1.2g fiber, 124mg cholesterol, 105mg sodium, 89mg potassium.

Orange Salad

Yield: 2 servings | **Prep time:** 5 minutes
Cook time: 0 minutes

Ingredients:

- 1 orange, peeled and chopped
- 1 tablespoon liquid honey
- 1 oz hazelnuts, chopped
- ½ teaspoon coconut shred
- 1 orange, peeled and chopped

Directions:

1. Put all ingredients in the salad bowl and shake well.

per serving: 182 calories, 4.3g protein, 27.8g carbohydrates, 7.7g fat, 4.8g fiber, 0mg cholesterol, 1mg sodium, 365mg potassium.

Russet Potato Frittata

Yield: 4 servings | **Prep time:** 5 minutes
Cook time: 10 minutes

Ingredients:

- 1 cup russet potato, peeled, chopped, and cooked
- 1 tablespoon avocado oil
- 4 oz salmon fillet, sliced
- 4 eggs, beaten
- 1 teaspoon fresh parsley, chopped

Directions:

1. Put all ingredients in the pan and transfer it to the preheated 365F oven.
2. Cook the frittata for 10 minutes.

per serving: 157 calories, 11.8g protein, 6.4g carbohydrates, 9.7g fat, 0.7g fiber, 176mg cholesterol, 77mg sodium, 347mg potassium.

Fragrant Garlic Salad

Yield: 2 servings | **Prep time:** 5 minutes
Cook time: 10 minutes

Ingredients:

- 1 cup white mushrooms, sliced
- 1 tablespoon avocado oil
- ½ teaspoon garlic, minced
- ½ teaspoon salt
- 14 teaspoons dried oregano
- 1 cup tomatoes, chopped
- 1 cup fresh spinach, chopped

Directions:

1. Roast the mushrooms with avocado oil for 10 minutes over medium heat. Stir them from time to time.
2. Then add garlic, salt, and oregano.
3. Transfer the mushrooms to the salad bowl.
4. Add all remaining ingredients and shake well.

per serving: 93 calories, 2.6g protein, 5.9g carbohydrates, 7.4g fat, 1.9g fiber, 0mg cholesterol, 600mg sodium, 434mg potassium.

Apple Quinoa

Yield: 4 servings | **Prep time:** 10 minutes
Cook time: 10 minutes

Ingredients:

- 1 cup apples, chopped
- 1 tablespoon liquid honey
- 2 cups coconut milk
- ½ cup quinoa
- 1 teaspoon vanilla extract

Directions:

1. Mix up quinoa and coconut milk in the saucepan. Cook the ingredients for 10 minutes.
2. Then add vanilla extract, honey, and apples.
3. Stir the meal well.

per serving: 163 calories, 6.9g protein, 30.6g carbohydrates, 1.6g fat, 8.7g fiber, 0mg cholesterol, 72mg sodium, 293mg potassium.

Eggs with Tender Chicken

Yield: 3 servings | **Prep time:** 10 minutes
Cook time: 15 minutes

Ingredients:

- 2 tablespoons olive oil
- 1 cup sweet potatoes, boiled and chopped
- ½ cup fresh dill, chopped
- 2 oz chicken fillet, finely chopped
- 4 eggs, beaten
- 2 oz Mozzarella cheese, shredded

Directions:

1. Heat the olive oil in the skillet and add chicken.
2. Cook it for 5 minutes.
3. Then stir the chicken and add eggs, sweet potato, and dill. Stir the mixture well and cook for 5 minutes more.
4. Then top the meal with cheese and cook it for 5 minutes over medium-low heat.

per serving: 331 calories, 18.6g protein, 15.3g carbohydrates, 22.2g fat, 2.4g fiber, 253mg cholesterol, 222mg sodium, 696mg potassium.

Beans and Seeds Salad

Yield: 4 servings | **Prep time:** 10 minutes
Cook time: 0 minutes

Ingredients:

- ½ cup red kidney beans, boiled
- 3 oz pumpkin seeds
- 1 tablespoon sesame seeds
- 2 teaspoons avocado oil
- 1 teaspoon liquid honey
- 1 cup Greek yogurt
- 1 cup blackberries

Directions:

1. Mix beans and Greek yogurt.
2. Then add avocado oil, sesame seeds, pumpkin seeds, honey, and blackberries.
3. Stir the meal well.

per serving: 272 calories, 17.6g protein, 25.4g carbohydrates, 12.4g fat, 10.2g fiber, 3mg cholesterol, 24mg sodium, 556mg potassium.

Fish Muffins

Yield: 5 servings | **Prep time:** 10 minutes
Cook time: 10 minutes

Ingredients:

- 5 eggs, beaten
- 10 oz canned tuna, drained and flaked
- 1 teaspoon dried cilantro
- ¼ teaspoon salt
- 2 oz Mozzarella cheese, shredded

Directions:

1. Mix up all ingredients in the bowl.
2. Then transfer the mixture to the muffin molds.
3. Bake the muffins for 10 minutes at 365F.

per serving: 213 calories, 23.6g protein, 1g carbohydrates, 12.7g fat, 0.1g fiber, 193mg cholesterol, 277mg sodium, 264mg potassium.

Feta Frittata

Yield: 4 servings | **Prep time:** 10 minutes
Cook time: 15 minutes

Ingredients:

- 5 oz salmon, boiled, shredded
- 4 eggs, beaten
- 5 oz feta cheese, crumbled
- 1 teaspoon avocado oil

Directions:

1. Heat avocado oil in the skillet.
2. Mix up all ingredients in the bowl.
3. Pour the egg liquid into the hot skillet and close the lid.
4. Cook the frittata for 13 minutes over medium heat.

per serving: 214 calories, 23.5g protein, 0.7g carbohydrates, 12.9g fat, 0.1g fiber, 193mg cholesterol, 277mg sodium, 264mg potassium.

Salmon Sandwich

Yield: 2 servings | **Prep time:** 5 minutes
Cook time: 0 minutes

Ingredients:

- 3 oz salmon, boiled
- 1 tablespoon plain yogurt
- ½ cup fresh spinach, chopped
- 4 whole-grain bread slices
- 2 Provolone cheese slices

Directions:

1. Mix up salmon, yogurt, and spinach.
2. Then spread 2 bread slices with salmon mixture and top with cheese.
3. Top the cheese with the remaining bread slices.

per serving: 340 calories, 25g protein, 29.9g carbohydrates, 14.8g fat, 4.2g fiber, 43mg cholesterol, 467mg sodium, 229mg potassium.

Blueberries Salad

Yield: 4 servings | **Prep time:** 5 minutes
Cook time: 0 minutes

Ingredients:

- ½ cup peach, pitted, chopped
- 1 mango, peeled and chopped
- ½ cup blueberries
- 1 tablespoon hemp seeds
- 1 tablespoon liquid honey

Directions:

1. Put all ingredients in the salad bowl and mix them.

per serving: 93 calories, 2.3g protein, 19.7g carbohydrates, 0.8g fat, 2.7g fiber, 0mg cholesterol, 1mg sodium, 207mg potassium.

Oat Muffins

Yield: 6 servings | **Prep time:** 10 minutes
Cook time: 15 minutes

Ingredients:

- 1 cup cut oats, cooked
- 3 eggs, beaten
- ¼ cup mozzarella, shredded
- 1 teaspoon olive oil
- 1 teaspoon ground paprika
- ¼ cup cream cheese

Directions:

1. Mix up all ingredients in the bowl.
2. Then transfer it to the muffin molds.
3. Bake the muffins for 15 minutes at 360F.

per serving: 198 calories, 7.9g protein, 18.6g carbohydrates, 8.3g fat, 2g fiber, 93mg cholesterol, 68mg sodium, 202mg potassium.

ANTIPASTI & TAPAS

Antipasti and Tapas

Oregano Beets

Yield: 6 serving | **Prep time:** 10 minutes
Cook time: 4 minutes

Ingredients:

- 1-pound beets, sliced, peeled
- 2 tablespoons lime juice
- 1 teaspoon dried oregano
- ¼ teaspoon garlic powder
- 1 tablespoon olive oil

Directions:

1. Sprinkle the beets with lime juice, oregano, garlic powder, and olive oil.
2. Then preheat the grill to 400F.
3. Place the sliced beet on the grill and cook it for 2 minutes per side.

per serving: 68 calories, 1.2g protein, 8g carbohydrates, 2.5g fat, 1.6g fiber, 0mg cholesterol, 59mg sodium, 242mg potassium.

Hot Salsa

Yield: 16 servings | **Prep time:** 40 minutes
Cook time: 0 minutes

Ingredients:

- 3 cups tomatoes, chopped
- 1 teaspoon salt
- 1 teaspoon chili powder
- ½ cup red onion, chopped
- 1 cup fresh parsley, chopped
- 1 jalapeno pepper, chopped
- 1 tablespoon olive oil
- 1 tablespoon apple cider vinegar

Directions:

1. Put all ingredients in the salad bowl and mix well.
2. Leave the cooked salsa for 30 minutes in the fridge.

per serving: 15 calories, 0.5g protein, 1.9g carbohydrates, 1g fat, 0.6g fiber, 0mg cholesterol, 150mg sodium, 95mg potassium.

Chives Dip

Yield: 4 servings | **Prep time:** 5 minutes
Cook time: 15 minutes

Ingredients:

- 1 cup spinach, chopped
- 2 oz chives, chopped
- ¼ cup plain yogurt
- ¼ teaspoon ground nutmeg
- 1 teaspoon olive oil

Directions:

1. Melt the olive oil in the saucepan.
2. Add spinach and chives.
3. Saute the greens for 10 minutes.
4. Then add ground nutmeg and plain yogurt. Stir well and cook it for 5 minutes more.
5. Then blend the mixture with the help of the immersion blender.

per serving: 30 calories, 0.5g protein, 3g carbohydrates, 1.4g fat, 0.6g fiber, 1mg cholesterol, 21mg sodium, 125mg potassium.

Feta Dip

Yield: 10 servings | **Prep time:** 10 minutes
Cook time: 0 minutes

Ingredients:

- 1-pound artichoke hearts, diced
- ¾ cup spinach, chopped
- 6 oz feta cheese, crumbled
- 1 teaspoon dried thyme
- ½ teaspoon garlic powder
- ¼ cup coconut milk

Directions:

1. Put all ingredients in the blender bowl and blend until smooth.

per serving: 47 calories, 2.3g protein, 5.6g carbohydrates, 2.2g fat, 2.6g fiber, 2mg cholesterol, 63mg sodium, 199mg potassium.

Cream Cheese Dip

Yield: 8 servings | **Prep time:** 10 minutes
Cook time: 0 minutes

Ingredients:

- 4 oz cream cheese
- ¼ teaspoon ground paprika
- ¼ teaspoon salt
- 2 avocados, peeled, pitted
- 1 teaspoon avocado oil
- ½ teaspoon lime juice
- 2 tablespoons fresh parsley, chopped

Directions:

1. Put all ingredients in the blender and blend until smooth.
2. Store the dip in the closed vessel in the fridge for up to 5 days.

per serving: 140 calories, 1.6g protein, 8g carbohydrates, 13.4g fat, 3.4g fiber, 6mg cholesterol, 85mg sodium, 272mg potassium.

Yogurt Dip

Yield: 4 servings | **Prep time:** 10 minutes
Cook time: 8 minutes

Ingredients:

- 3 oz goats cheese, soft
- 2 oz Greek yogurt
- 2 oz scallions, chopped
- 1 tablespoon lemon juice
- ¼ teaspoon ground black pepper
- 2 bell peppers

Directions:

1. Grill the bell peppers for 3-4 minutes per side.
2. Then peel the peppers and remove the seeds.
3. Then put bell peppers in the blender.
4. Add all remaining ingredients, blend them well, and transfer them to the ramekins.

per serving: 94 calories, 6g protein, 6.5g carbohydrates, 4.9g fat, 1.3g fiber, 11mg cholesterol, 91mg sodium, 198mg potassium.

Greens Antipasti

Yield: 8 servings | **Prep time:** 5 minutes
Cook time: 0 minutes

Ingredients:

- 2 oz chives, chopped
- 1 cup arugula, chopped
- 2 cups green lentils, boiled
- 1 chili pepper, chopped
- 1 tablespoon avocado oil
- 1 teaspoon lemon juice

Directions:

1. Put all ingredients in the bowl and stir well.

per serving: 187 calories, 9.8g protein, 30.9g carbohydrates, 3.2g fat, 9.1g fiber, 0mg cholesterol, 13mg sodium, 479mg potassium.

Cinnamon Antipasti

Yield: 6 servings | **Prep time:** 10 minutes
Cook time: 0 minutes

Ingredients:

- 1 teaspoon ground cinnamon
- 1 cup fresh dill, chopped
- 1 tablespoon lime juice
- 3 tablespoons avocado oil
- 2 oz celery stalk, chopped

Directions:

1. Mix all ingredients in the bowl and leave for 5 minutes in the fridge.

per serving: 17 calories, 0.6g protein, 1.7g carbohydrates, 1g fat, 0.8g fiber, 0mg cholesterol, 14mg sodium, 110mg potassium

Cilantro Tapas

Yield: 8 servings | **Prep time:** 5 minutes
Cook time: 0 minutes

Ingredients:

- ½ teaspoon garlic, minced
- 2 cups plain yogurt
- ½ cup fresh cilantro, chopped
- ¼ teaspoon ground black pepper
- 2 pecans, chopped
- 2 tablespoon lime juice

Directions:

1. Put all ingredients in the bowl and stir well with the help of the spoon.

per serving: 78 calories, 4.5g protein, 6.3g carbohydrates, 3.4g fat, 0.8g fiber, 4mg cholesterol, 50mg sodium, 264mg potassium.

Cheddar Spread

Yield: 6 servings | **Prep time:** 10 minutes
Cook time: 8 minutes

Ingredients:

- ½ cup Cheddar cheese, grated
- 3 tablespoons Greek yogurt
- 1 mini cucumber, grated
- 1 oz fresh dill, chopped
- ¼ teaspoon ground paprika

Directions:

1. Carefully mix yogurt, Cheddar cheese, dill, and ground paprika.
2. Then add grated cucumber and gently mix the spread.

per serving: 85 calories, 2.5g protein, 3.5g carbohydrates, 7g fat, 0.8g fiber, 21mg cholesterol, 198mg sodium, 185mg potassium.

Lime Beans

Yield: 8 servings | **Prep time:** 10 minutes
Cook time: 0 minutes

Ingredients:

- 2 cups cannellini beans, boiled
- 1 tablespoon chives, chopped
- 3 tablespoons olive oil
- ¼ teaspoon ground coriander
- 1 tablespoon lime juice
- ½ teaspoon lime zest, grated

- 3 oz beef, chopped, cooked

Directions:

1. Put all ingredients in the bowl and stir well.

per serving: 2225 calories, 14.1g protein, 28 carbohydrates, 6.3g fat, 11.5g fiber, 10mg cholesterol, 19mg sodium, 694mg potassium.

Basil Chips

Yield: 6 servings | **Prep time:** 5 minutes
Cook time: 10 minutes

Ingredients:

- 2 carrots, thinly sliced
- 1 teaspoon dried basil
- 1 teaspoon avocado oil

Directions:

1. Line the baking tray with baking paper.
2. Then arrange the sliced carrot in one layer.
3. Sprinkle the vegetables with avocado oil and basil.
4. Bake the carrot chips for 10 minutes or until the vegetables are crunchy.

per serving: 16 calories, 0.2g protein, 2g carbohydrates, 0.8g fat, 0.5g fiber, 0mg cholesterol, 403mg sodium, 65mg potassium.

Olives Antipasti

Yield: 4 servings | **Prep time:** 10 minutes
Cook time: 0 minutes

Ingredients:

- ½ cup black olives, pitted and sliced
- 1 cucumber, spiralized
- 1 cup Roma tomatoes, chopped
- 4 oz Goat cheese, crumbled
- 2 tablespoons olive oil

Directions:

1. Put black olives, spiralized cucumber, and tomatoes in the bowl.
2. Add olive oil and stir well.
3. Then top the salad with Goat cheese.

per serving: 184 calories, 4.9g protein, 6.7g carbohydrates, 16.3g fat, 0.9g fiber, 25mg cholesterol, 464mg sodium, 234mg potassium.

Chickpea Spread

Yield: 10 servings | **Prep time:** 10 minutes
Cook time: 0 minutes

Ingredients:

- 3 cups Kalamata olives, pitted
- ½ cup chickpeas, boiled

- 1 teaspoon dried oregano
- 3 tablespoons olive oil
- ½ teaspoon ground black pepper

Directions:

1. Put all ingredients in the blender and blend until smooth.

per serving: 132 calories, 2.1g protein, 8.7g carbohydrates, 9.3g fat, 3.1g fiber, 1.2mg cholesterol, 354mg sodium, 93mg potassium.

Parsley Antipasti

Yield: 6 servings | **Prep time:** 10 minutes
Cook time: 4 minutes

Ingredients:

- 5 sweet peppers, trimmed
- 1 tablespoon avocado oil
- 3 tablespoons sunflower oil
- ½ teaspoon salt
- 2 garlic cloves, minced
- 3 tablespoons fresh parsley, chopped

Directions:

1. Pierce the sweet peppers with the help of a knife and sprinkle them with avocado oil.
2. Grill the vegetables at 400F for 2 minutes per side.
3. Then peel them and remove the seeds.
4. Put the grilled bell peppers in the blender and add all remaining ingredients.
5. Blend the mixture well.

per serving: 63 calories, 1.2g protein, 8.2g carbohydrates, 3.5g fat, 1.7g fiber, 0mg cholesterol, 197mg sodium, 215mg potassium.

Tomato Rings

Yield: 4 servings | **Prep time:** 10 minutes
Cook time: 0 minutes

Ingredients:

- ½ cup hummus
- 2 Roma tomatoes

Directions:

1. Roughly slice the tomatoes.
2. Then fill every tomato ring with hummus.

per serving: 74 calories, 3.5g protein, 9.9g carbohydrates, 3.2g fat, 2.6g fiber, 0mg cholesterol, 121mg sodium, 292mg potassium.

Cucumber Slices

Yield: 4 servings | **Prep time:** 10 minutes
Cook time: 0 minutes

Ingredients:

- 1 cucumber, sliced
- 1 teaspoon lemon juice
- 2 tablespoons Greek yogurt
- 1 teaspoon dried parsley
- 3 oz salmon, smoked, sliced

Directions:

1. Arrange the sliced cucumber on the plate in one layer.
2. Then sprinkle them with lemon juice, Greek yogurt, and dried parsley.
3. Then top the cucumbers with sliced salmon.

per serving: 35 calories, 4.6g protein, 0.8g carbohydrates, 1.4g fat, 0.1g fiber, 10mg cholesterol, 15mg sodium, 109mg potassium.

Mozzarella Balls

Yield: 8 servings | **Prep time:** 10 minutes
Cook time: 5 minutes

Ingredients:

- 2 zucchinis, grilled
- 2 tablespoons olive oil
- 1 garlic clove, minced
- 1 egg, beaten
- ½ cup oatmeal, ground
- ½ teaspoon ground black pepper
- 2 oz Mozzarella, grated

Directions:

1. Blend the zucchini until smooth.
2. Then mix up blended zucchini with garlic, egg, oatmeal, ground black pepper, and Mozzarella.
3. Make the small balls.
4. Heat the skillet with olive oil and put the zucchini balls inside.
5. Roast them on high heat for 1 minute per side.

per serving: 115 calories, 5g protein, 12g carbohydrates, 5.2g fat, 5.4g fiber, 26mg cholesterol, 77mg sodium, 343mg potassium.

Basil Zucchini Chips

Yield: 10 servings | **Prep time:** 10 minutes
Cook time: 5 minutes

Ingredients:

- 2 zucchinis, thinly sliced
- 1 teaspoon ground black pepper
- 1 teaspoon dried basil
- 1 tablespoon olive oil

Directions:

1. Rub the zucchinis slices with ground black pepper and basil.
2. Then sprinkle the vegetable slices with olive oil.
3. Grill the zucchini slices for 2 minutes per side at 400F or until the vegetables are crunchy.

per serving: 41 calories, 1.1g protein, 6.6g carbohydrates, 1.8g fat, 3.9g fiber, 0mg cholesterol, 2mg sodium, 254mg potassium.

Parmesan Dip

Yield: 7 servings | **Prep time:** 10 minutes
Cook time: 0 minutes

Ingredients:

- 1 cup red lentils, cooked
- 1 tablespoon lemon juice
- 1 tomato, chopped
- 1 teaspoon avocado oil
- 2 oz Parmesan, grated

Directions:

1. Mix up all ingredients in the bowl and blend gently with the help of the immersion blender.

per serving: 131 calories, 9.8g protein, 17.1g carbohydrates, 2.7g fat, 8.5g fiber, 6mg cholesterol, 77mg sodium, 285mg potassium.

Garlic Baby Potatoes

Yield: 2 servings | **Prep time:** 10 minutes
Cook time: 20 minutes

Ingredients:

- 4 baby potatoes
- 2 oz Parmesan cheese, shredded
- ¼ teaspoon garlic, minced
- 1 teaspoon avocado oil

Directions:

1. Cut the baby potatoes into halves and sprinkle them with garlic and avocado oil.
2. Bake the potatoes for 10 minutes at 365F.
3. Then top them with Parmesan cheese and bake for 10 minutes more.

per serving: 136 calories, 7.7g protein, 4.5g carbohydrates, 9.7g fat, 0.4g fiber, 30mg cholesterol, 177mg sodium, 39mg potassium.

Fish and Cream Cheese Paste

Yield: 6 servings | **Prep time:** 5 minutes
Cook time: 0 minutes

Ingredients:

- 7 oz tuna, canned, drained
- 2 tablespoons mascarpone
- 1 tablespoon scallions, chopped

Directions:

1. Put all ingredients in the bowl and stir well with the help of the fork.

per serving: 73 calories, 9g protein, 0.1g carbohydrates, 3.8g fat, 0g fiber, 14mg cholesterol, 26mg sodium, 116mg potassium.

Butternut Squash Chips

Yield: 10 servings | **Prep time:** 5 minutes
Cook time: 12 minutes

Ingredients:

- 10 oz butternut squash, thinly sliced
- 1 oz Parmesan, grated

Directions:

1. Line the baking tray with baking paper.
2. Put the butternut squash in the tray in one layer and top with Parmesan.
3. Bake the chips for 12 minutes at 375F.

per serving: 15 calories, 1.4g protein, 1.4g carbohydrates, 0.7g fat, 0.4g fiber, 2mg cholesterol, 30mg sodium, 103mg potassium.

Greece Style Chickpeas

Yield: 2 servings | **Prep time:** 5 minutes
Cook time: 10 minutes

Ingredients:

- ¼ cup chickpeas, boiled
- 1 tablespoon olive oil
- 1 teaspoon ground paprika
- 1 oz Parmesan, grated

Directions:

1. Line the baking tray with baking paper.
2. Mix up chickpeas with ground paprika and olive oil and transfer the mixture to the tray. Flatten it gently.
3. Bake the chickpeas for 10 minutes at 400F. Stir them every 2 minutes.
4. Then top the cooked chickpeas with Parmesan.

per serving: 103 calories, 5.1g protein, 16.1g carbohydrates, 2.5g fat, 5.1g fiber, 0mg cholesterol, 7mg sodium, 265mg potassium.

Pecan Dates

Yield: 4 servings | **Prep time:** 5 minutes
Cook time: 0 minutes

Ingredients:

- 4 dates, pitted
- 4 pecans

Directions:

1. Fill the dates with pecans.

per serving: 76 calories, 1.5g protein, 7g carbohydrates, 5.1g fat, 1.4g fiber, 0mg cholesterol, 0mg sodium, 54mg potassium.

SOUPS

Soups

Kofte Soup

Yield: 4 servings | **Prep time:** 10 minutes
Cook time: 30 minutes

Ingredients:

- 1 cup pork loin, minced
- ½ teaspoon ground black pepper
- 1 garlic clove, minced
- 1 teaspoon ground coriander
- 1 onion, diced
- 1 teaspoon olive oil
- 3 cups chicken stock

Directions:

1. Heat the olive oil in the saucepan.
2. Add diced onion and cook it for 3 minutes. Transfer the onion to the pan.
3. Meanwhile, mix up minced pork, ground black pepper, minced garlic, and ground coriander.
4. Make the round balls – koftes.
5. Pour the chicken stock into the onion and bring it to a boil.
6. Add koftes and cook the soup for 10 minutes over medium heat.

per serving: 139 calories, 22.7g protein, 3.9g carbohydrates, 3.6g fat, 0.8g fiber, 61mg cholesterol, 622mg sodium, 412mg potassium.

Mozzarella Soup

Yield: 4 servings | **Prep time:** 10 minutes
Cook time: 10 minutes

Ingredients:

- 3 oz scallions, chopped
- 1 tablespoon avocado oil
- 4 cups chicken stock
- 2 eggs, beaten
- 2 cups snap peas, frozen
- 1 oz Mozzarella, grated

Directions:

1. Heat a saucepan with avocado oil over medium-high heat, add scallions, stir, and cook for 2 minutes.
2. Add stock and bring to a boil.
3. Add eggs and all remaining ingredients to the soup.
4. Cook it for 7 minutes more.

per serving: 162 calories, 10g protein, 13.9g carbohydrates, 8g fat, 4.3g fiber, 87mg cholesterol, 865mg sodium, 259mg potassium.

Rice Soup

Yield: 4 servings | **Prep time:** 10 minutes
Cook time: 25 minutes

Ingredients:

- ¼ cup long-grain rice
- 4 cups chicken stock
- ½ cup Provolone cheese, shredded
- ¼ teaspoon ground black pepper
- ½ teaspoon dried basil
- ½ cup peas, frozen

Directions:

1. Heat a saucepan with the stock.
2. Add all ingredients except provolone cheese and bring the soup to a boil.
3. Then add cheese and stir it well.
4. Cook the soup for 5 minutes over low heat.

per serving: 95 calories, 5.4g protein, 6.1g carbohydrates, 5.5g fat, 1g fiber, 15mg cholesterol, 853mg sodium, 78mg potassium.

Mercimek Soup

Yield: 5 servings | **Prep time:** 5 minutes
Cook time: 35 minutes

Ingredients:

- 8 cups water
- 1 cup red lentils
- 1 onion, diced
- 1 tablespoon lemon juice
- 1 tablespoon tomato paste
- 1 teaspoon chili powder
- 1 teaspoon olive oil

Directions:

1. Melt olive oil in the saucepan and add onion.
2. Roast the onion for 5 minutes.
3. After this, add red lentils, tomato paste, chili powder, lemon juice, and chicken broth. Stir the soup well.
4. Cook the soup for 30 minutes over medium heat.

per serving: 225 calories, 18.4g protein, 29.3g carbohydrates, 3.7g fat, 12.8g fiber, 0mg cholesterol, 1233mg sodium, 816mg potassium.

Cabbage Soup

Yield: 4 servings | **Prep time:** 10 minutes
Cook time: 20 minutes

Ingredients:

- 1 cup green cabbage, chopped
- ¼ teaspoon salt
- ¼ teaspoon white pepper
- 1 tablespoon olive oil

1 oz celery stalk, diced
¼ cup carrot, grated
1 cup tomatoes, chopped
4 cups water

Directions:

1. Put all ingredients except cabbage in the pan and bring to a boil.
2. Then add cabbage, stir the soup, and cook it for 5 minutes over medium heat.

per serving: 60 calories, 1.7g protein, 5.2g carbohydrates, 4.1g fat, 1.1g fiber, 0mg cholesterol, 931mg sodium, 246mg potassium

Watermelon Gazpacho

Yield: 5 servings | **Prep time:** 10 minutes
Cook time: 0 minutes

Ingredients:

- 1-pound watermelon, peeled, chopped
- 1 tablespoon olive oil
- 1 red onion, diced
- ¼ cup of water
- 1 teaspoon dried basil

Directions:

1. Put all ingredients in the blender and blend until smooth.
2. Pour the cooked gazpacho into the serving bowls.

per serving: 43 calories, 1g protein, 9.6g carbohydrates, 0.6g fat, 1.4g fiber, 0mg cholesterol, 16mg sodium, 284mg potassium.

Dill Soup

Yield: 6 servings | **Prep time:** 10 minutes
Cook time: 30 minutes

Ingredients:

- 1-pound chicken breast, skinless, boneless, chopped
- ½ cup fresh dill, chopped
- ½ teaspoon ground black pepper
- 1 onion, diced
- 1 teaspoon avocado oil
- 6 cups of water

Directions:

1. Preheat the avocado oil in the pan and add the onion.
2. Cook it until light brown.
3. Add chicken breast, dill, and ground black pepper.
4. Add water and simmer the soup for 25 minutes.

per serving: 102 calories, 16.4g protein, 2.2g carbohydrates, 2.7g fat, 0.6g fiber, 48mg cholesterol, 42mg sodium, 336mg potassium.

Shrimp Soup

Yield: 6 servings | **Prep time:** 10 minutes
Cook time: 15 minutes

Ingredients:

- 1 cup sweet pepper, chopped
- 1 cup tomatoes, chopped
- 2 tablespoons avocado oil
- ½ teaspoon garlic, minced
- 1-pound shrimp, peeled
- ½ teaspoon ground coriander
- 5 cups of water

Directions:

1. Roast the sweet peppers with avocado oil in the pan for 5 minutes.
2. Add tomatoes, garlic, shrimp, and ground coriander.
3. Then add water and close the lid.
4. Simmer the soup for 5 minutes.

per serving: 141 calories, 17.7 g protein, 4g carbohydrates, 5.9g fat, 0.7g fiber, 159mg cholesterol, 192mg sodium, 241mg potassium.

Hazelnut Gazpacho

Yield: 4 servings | **Prep time:** 15 minutes
Cook time: 0 minutes

Ingredients:

- ½ cup hazelnuts
- 1 cup cucumbers, chopped
- 1 tomato, chopped
- 3 oz water, warm
- 2 oz chives, chopped
- 1 tablespoon olive oil
- ¼ cup fresh dill, chopped
- ¼ cup plain yogurt

Directions:

1. Put all ingredients in the blender and blend until smooth.
2. Cool the cooked gazpacho in the fridge for 10-15 minutes.

per serving: 127 calories, 4.6g protein, 7g carbohydrates, 9.9g fat, 2.4g fiber, 1mg cholesterol, 19mg sodium, 304mg potassium.

Celery Stalk Soup

Yield: 4 servings | **Prep time:** 10 minutes
Cook time: 25 minutes

Ingredients:

- 3 cups water
- 7 oz chicken fillet, chopped
- 1 tablespoon chives, chopped

- ¼ cup fresh dill, chopped
- 2 oz celery stalk, chopped
- ¼ cup plain yogurt
- ½ teaspoon salt
- 1 teaspoon chili powder

Directions:

1. Bring the water to boil and the chicken fillet.
2. Simmer the chicken for 5 minutes.
3. After this, add all remaining ingredients, stir the soup, and cook it for 20 minutes.

per serving: 124 calories, 16.5g protein, 4.1g carbohydrates, 4.5g fat, 0.8g fiber, 45mg cholesterol, 935mg sodium, 317mg potassium.

Jalapeno Soup

Yield: 6 servings | **Prep time:** 10 minutes
Cook time: 25minutes

Ingredients:

- 6 cups beef broth
- 1 cup long-grain rice
- 4 oz fennel, diced
- 1 teaspoon salt
- ½ teaspoon ground paprika
- 1 jalapeno pepper, chopped
- 1 tablespoon olive oil

Directions:

1. Heat the olive oil in the saucepan.
2. Add fennel and roast it for 5 minutes.
3. Then add all remaining ingredients and close the lid.
4. Simmer the soup for 20 minutes over medium heat.

per serving: 161 calories, 7.4g protein, 27.3g carbohydrates, 1.9g fat, 1.2g fiber, 0mg cholesterol, 1162mg sodium, 337mg potassium.

Red Soup

Yield: 4 servings | **Prep time:** 10 minutes
Cook time: 15 minutes

Ingredients:

- 2 cups tomatoes, chopped
- 1 cup chicken stock
- 1 teaspoon cayenne pepper
- 1 teaspoon dried oregano
- 1 teaspoon ground paprika
- 1 oz Parmesan, grated

Directions:

1. Blend the tomatoes and pour the mixture into the saucepan.
2. Add all remaining ingredients except Parmesan and bring the soup to a boil.

3. Then ladle the cooked soup into the bowls and top with Parmesan.

per serving: 69 calories, 5.9g protein, 6.1g carbohydrates 2.9g fat, 1.9g fiber, 7mg cholesterol, 348mg sodium 383mg potassium.

Yogurt Soup

Yield: 4 servings | **Prep time:** 5 minutes
Cook time: 30 minutes

Ingredients:

- 8 oz chicken fillet, cut into strips
- 2 tablespoons fresh parsley, chopped
- 1 cup Greek yogurt
- 2 cups of water
- 1 teaspoon chili flakes

Directions:

1. Put all ingredients in the pan and simmer for 30 minutes on low heat.

per serving: 152 calories, 19.9g protein, 4.4g carbohydrates, 5g fat, 0g fiber, 54mg cholesterol, 95mg sodium, 286mg potassium.

Corn and Tomatillos Soup

Yield: 4 servings | **Prep time:** 10 minutes
Cook time: 25 minutes

Ingredients:

- 2 cups tomatillos, chopped
- 1 yellow onion, diced
- ½ cup bell pepper, chopped
- 1 tablespoon olive oil
- ½ teaspoon salt
- ½ teaspoon ground turmeric
- 4 cups water
- ½ cup corn kernels, frozen

Directions:

1. Roast the onion with bell pepper and olive oil in the saucepan for 5 minutes.
2. Then add tomatillos, salt, ground turmeric, and water.
3. Bring the liquid to a boil and then blend with the help of the immersion blender.
4. Add corn kernels and simmer the soup for 10 minutes more.

per serving: 87 calories, 5.4g protein, 12.2g carbohydrates, 2.5g fat, 2.8g fiber, 0mg cholesterol 870mg sodium, 467mg potassium.

Red Kidney Beans Soup

Yield: 4 servings | **Prep time:** 10 minutes
Cook time: 40 minutes

Ingredients:

- 5 oz beef tenderloin, sliced
- 1 chili pepper, chopped
- 1 ½ cups red kidney beans, soaked
- 5 cups of water
- 1 teaspoon salt
- 2 tablespoons tomato paste

Directions:

1. Put all ingredients in the saucepan and stir until tomato paste is dissolved.
2. Close the lid and cook the soup for 40 minutes over medium-low heat.

per serving: 332 calories, 28.3 g protein, 47.2g carbohydrates, 3.9g fat, 11.8g fiber, 33mg cholesterol, 631mg sodium, 1571mg potassium.

Broccoli Cream Soup

Yield: 4 servings | **Prep time:** 10 minutes
Cook time: 20 minutes

Ingredients:

- 2 cups broccoli, chopped
- 1 cup Plain yogurt
- 3 cups of water
- 1 onion, diced
- 1 teaspoon ground paprika
- ¼ cup Cheddar cheese, shredded

Directions:

1. Put all ingredients except Cheddar cheese in the pan.
2. Bring the mixture to a boil and simmer it for 15 minutes.
3. After this, blend the soup with the help of the immersion blender, add cheese, and cook it for 5 minutes more.

per serving: 97 calories, 6.6g protein, 10g carbohydrates, 3.2g fat, 2g fiber, 11mg cholesterol, 108mg sodium, 350mg potassium.

Eggplant Soup

Yield: 4 servings | **Prep time:** 10 minutes
Cook time: 10 minutes

Ingredients:

- 2 eggplants, peeled and chopped
- 2 tablespoons Greek yogurt
- 1 teaspoon dried basil
- 3 cups chicken stock
- 2 oz Parmesan, grated

Directions:

1. Pour chicken stock into the pan.
2. Add basil and Greek yogurt and bring the liquid to a boil.
3. Add chopped eggplants and remove the soup from the heat.
4. Leave it for 10 minutes.
5. After this, add Parmesan and stir the soup gently.

per serving: 77 calories, 7.3g protein, 5g carbohydrates, 3.9g fat, 1.2g fiber, 11mg cholesterol, 717mg sodium, 288mg potassium

Pepper Soup

Yield: 4 servings | **Prep time:** 10 minutes
Cook time: 30 minutes

Ingredients:

- 6 oz beef loin, chopped
- 4 oz whole-grain pasta
- 5 cups of water
- 2 bell pepper, chopped
- ½ teaspoon salt

Directions:

1. Pour water into the pan and bring it to a boil.
2. Add beef loin, peppers, and salt. Simmer the beef for 15 minutes.
3. Then add pasta and cook the soup for 10 minutes more.

per serving: 260 calories, 18.1g protein, 39.3g carbohydrates, 3.1g fat, 7.1g fiber, 27mg cholesterol, 332mg sodium, 167mg potassium.

Shiitake Mushrooms Soup

Yield: 2 servings | **Prep time:** 10 minutes
Cook time: 25 minutes

Ingredients:

- 4 oz Shiitake mushrooms, chopped
- 3 oz Parmesan cheese, shredded
- ½ cup white onion, diced
- 1 teaspoon cayenne pepper
- 1 tablespoon olive oil
- 2 cups of water

Directions:

1. Melt the olive oil in the pan and add onion and mushrooms.
2. Cook the vegetables for 5 minutes over medium heat.
3. Then add cayenne pepper and water.
4. Simmer the soup for 10 minutes.

5. Add Parmesan cheese and stir the soup until the cheese is melted.
6. Remove the soup from the heat.

per serving: 142 calories, 5.7g protein, 5.2g carbohydrates, 11.8g fat, 1.4g fiber, 15mg cholesterol, 100mg sodium, 257mg potassium.

Onion Soup

Yield: 2 servings | **Prep time:** 10 minutes
Cook time: 20 minutes

Ingredients:

- 5 oz celery stalk, diced
- 1 white onion, diced
- ½ cup cream cheese
- 2 cups water
- 1 teaspoon chili powder
- 1 tablespoon olive oil

Directions:

1. Melt the olive oil in the saucepan.
2. Add celery stalk and white onion and saute the vegetables for 10 minutes.
3. Then add cream cheese, chili powder, and water. Boil the soup for 5 minutes more.

per serving: 312 calories, 6.2g protein, 11.3g carbohydrates, 28.1g fat, 2g fiber, 64mg cholesterol, 955mg sodium, 229mg potassium.

Beef Soup

Yield: 4 servings | **Prep time:** 10 minutes
Cook time: 35 minutes

Ingredients:

- 9 oz beef sirloin, sliced
- 5 cups of water
- 1 cup broccoli, chopped
- ½ teaspoon ground black pepper
- 1 teaspoon dried dill
- 2 tablespoons tomato paste

Directions:

1. Preheat the pan well and add beef sirloin.
2. Roast it for 1 minute per side.
3. Then add water, ground black pepper, and dried dill.
4. Close the lid and cook the meat for 20 minutes.
5. Then add tomato paste and broccoli. Stir the soup.
6. Cook the soup for 10 minutes.

per serving: 144 calories, 19g protein, 3.2g carbohydrates, 5.9g fat, 1.1g fiber, 59mg cholesterol, 70mg sodium, 384mg potassium.

Fennel Soup

Yield: 4 servings | **Prep time:** 10 minutes
Cook time: 25 minutes

Ingredients:

- 2 zucchinis, chopped
- 1 tablespoon olive oil
- 1 teaspoon cayenne pepper
- ½ teaspoon dried rosemary
- 4 oz fennel bulb, chopped
- ½ cup red kidney beans, cooked
- 4 cups of water

Directions:

1. Heat olive oil in the saucepan and add zucchini.
2. Roast them for 1 minute per side.
3. Then add cayenne pepper, dried rosemary, a fennel bulb, red kidney beans, and water.
4. Close the lid and cook the soup on low heat for 20 minutes or until all ingredients are soft.

per serving: 186 calories, 8.6g protein, 32.1g carbohydrates, 4.4g fat, 13.9g fiber, 0mg cholesterol, 23mg sodium, 1025mg potassium.

Lime Soup

Yield: 2 servings | **Prep time:** 10 minutes
Cook time: 15 minutes

Ingredients:

- 2 tablespoons lime juice
- ½ teaspoon lime zest, grated
- ¼ cup long-grain rice
- 4 cups beef broth
- 1 celery stalk, chopped

Directions:

1. Bring the beef broth to a boil and add rice. Boil it for 10 minutes.
2. Then add lime zest and celery stalk. Cook the soup for 3 minutes more.
3. After this, add lime juice and boil it for 2 minutes.

per serving: 109 calories, 3.2g protein, 20.6g carbohydrates, 1.4g fat, 0.5g fiber, 0mg cholesterol, 1538mg sodium, 98mg potassium.

Carrot and Mint Soup

Yield: 4 servings | **Prep time:** 10 minutes
Cook time: 30 minutes

Ingredients:

- 1 teaspoon dried mint
- 2 cups carrot, chopped
- 1 onion, diced
- ½ cup plain yogurt

4 cups water
½ teaspoon dried dill
½ teaspoon chili flakes

Directions:

1. Put all ingredients in the saucepan and bring to a boil.
2. Then simmer the mixture for 25 minutes or until the carrot is soft.
3. With the help of the immersion blender blend the soup.
4. Simmer it for 5 minutes more.

per serving: 67 calories, 3.3g protein, 11.3g carbohydrates, 1g fat, 2. g fiber, 2mg cholesterol, 824mg sodium, 315mg potassium.

Cucumber Soup

Yield: 4 servings | **Prep time:** 10 minutes
Cook time: 0 minutes

Ingredients:

- 5 cucumbers, grated
- 1 teaspoon ground paprika
- ¼ teaspoon dried mint
- 3 cups plain yogurt
- 1 cup of water
- 1 teaspoon avocado oil

Directions:

1. Put all ingredients in the bowl and gently mix.

per serving: 277 calories, 34.7g protein, 14.5g carbohydrates, 6.3g fat, 0.5g fiber, 84mg cholesterol, 189mg sodium, 883mg potassium.

Red Macaroni Soup

Yield: 6 servings | **Prep time:** 10 minutes
Cook time: 20 minutes

Ingredients:

- 1 tablespoon olive oil
- 6 oz macaroni
- ½ cup tomatoes, chopped
- 5 cups water
- 1 tablespoon tomato paste
- 1 jalapeno pepper, chopped
- ½ cup Cheddar cheese, shredded

Directions:

1. Bring the water to a boil.
2. Add macaroni, chopped tomatoes, and jalapeno pepper.
3. Then add olive oil, and tomato paste, and simmer the soup for 15 minutes.
4. After this, ladle the cooked soup into the bowls and

top with Cheddar cheese.

per serving: 164 calories, 8.5g protein, 22.2g carbohydrates, 4.3g fat, 1.3g fiber, 10mg cholesterol, 713mg sodium, 230mg potassium.

Cauliflower Soup

Yield: 4 servings | **Prep time:** 10 minutes
Cook time: 20 minutes

Ingredients:

- 3 cups cauliflower, chopped
- 3 cups of water
- ½ cup Cheddar cheese, shredded
- 1 teaspoon cayenne pepper

Directions:

1. Mix the cauliflower and water in the pan and boil for 10 minutes or until the vegetables are soft.
2. Then cayenne pepper, and cheese.
3. Stir the soup well and bring it to a boil.
4. Then blend it with the help of the immersion blender until smooth.
5. Simmer the soup for 2 minutes more.

per serving: 735 calories, 3g protein, 4.9g carbohydrates, 0.9g fat, 1.9g fiber, 2mg cholesterol, 49mg sodium, 227mg potassium.

Sweet Potato Soup

Yield: 4 servings | **Prep time:** 10 minutes
Cook time: 30 minutes

Ingredients:

- 1-pound chicken fillet, roughly chopped
- 1 white onion, roughly chopped
- 2 sweet potatoes, chopped
- 1 tablespoon olive oil
- ½ teaspoon dried coriander
- ½ teaspoon dried thyme
- 4 cups of water

Directions:

1. Roast the chicken fillet in the saucepan with olive oil for 2 minutes per side.
2. Then add onion and sweet potatoes.
3. Keep cooking the ingredients for 3 minutes more.
4. After this, add the remaining ingredients and simmer the soup for 30 minutes.

per serving: 276 calories, 33.2g protein, 2.9g carbohydrates, 13.9g fat, 0.7g fiber, 104mg cholesterol, 75mg sodium, 456mg potassium.

Minced Chicken Soup

Yield: 2 servings | **Prep time:** 10 minutes
Cook time: 25 minutes

Ingredients:

- 3 oz chicken fillet, minced
- 1 teaspoon garlic, diced
- 1 tablespoon fresh parsley, chopped
- 1 bell pepper, chopped
- 1 tomato, chopped
- 1 tablespoon olive oil
- 3 cups of water

Directions:

1. Roast the minced chicken fillet in the saucepan with olive oil for 4 minutes. Stir the chicken occasionally.
2. Then add garlic, parsley, bell pepper, and tomato. Stir the ingredients well.
3. Add water and close the lid.
4. Simmer the soup for 20 minutes on medium heat.

per serving: 170 calories, 14.2g protein, 7g carbohydrates, 9.7g fat, 1.4g fiber, 38mg cholesterol, 45mg sodium, 417mg potassium.

Tender Green Peas Soup

Yield: 4 servings | **Prep time:** 10 minutes
Cook time: 30 minutes

Ingredients:

- 1 cup green peas, frozen
- 1 jalapeno pepper, sliced
- ¼ cup fresh dill, chopped
- 4 cups of water
- 6 oz beef sirloin, chopped
- 1 tablespoon olive oil

Directions:

1. Roast the beef with olive oil in the saucepan for 2 minutes per side.
2. Then add water and boil the meat for 20 minutes.
3. Add green peas, jalapeno pepper, and dill.
4. Close the lid and cook the soup for 10 minutes on low heat.

per serving: 144 calories, 14.3g protein, 7.7g carbohydrates, 6.6g fat, 1.3g fiber, 38mg cholesterol, 43mg sodium, 306mg potassium

Cannellini Beans Soup

Yield: 6 servings | **Prep time:** 10 minutes
Cook time: 35 minutes

Ingredients:

- 2 cups cannellini beans, boiled
- 4 cups chicken stock
- 1 cup chicken fillet, minced
- 1 teaspoon dried basil
- 1 tablespoon tomato paste
- 1 onion, diced
- 1 tablespoon olive oil

Directions:

1. Melt the olive oil in the saucepan.
2. Add onion and chicken. Cook the ingredients for 10 minutes.
3. Then add tomato paste, and basil, and stir well.
4. Add beans and chicken stock.
5. Close the lid and cook the soup for 25 minutes on medium heat.

per serving: 322 calories, 29.1g protein, 40.3g carbohydrates, 5.3g fat, 9.8g fiber, 41mg cholesterol, 552mg sodium, 1131mg potassium.

Creamy Asparagus Soup

Yield: 4 servings | **Prep time:** 5 minutes
Cook time: 25 minutes

Ingredients:

- 1-pound asparagus, chopped
- 4 cups water
- ½ cup cream
- 1 teaspoon chili powder
- 1 tablespoon cream cheese

Directions:

1. Put the sliced carrot in the pan.
2. Add water, cream cheese, cream, and chili powder.
3. Cook the soup for 15 minutes.
4. After this, add asparagus and simmer the soup for 10 minutes more.

per serving: 76 calories, 7.6g protein, 7.3g carbohydrates, 2.3g fat, 3g fiber, 1mg cholesterol, 784mg sodium, 501mg potassium.

Farro Soup

Yield: 6 servings | **Prep time:** 5 minutes
Cook time: 15 minutes

Ingredients:

- 1 cup farro
- 5 cups of water
- 1 cup chicken broth
- ¼ cup fresh dill, chopped
- 1 bell pepper, chopped
- 1 teaspoon chili flakes
- 1 zucchini, diced

Directions:

1. Bring the chicken broth to a boil.
2. Add bell pepper and chili flakes. Cook the ingredients for 5 minutes.
3. Then add all remaining ingredients, stir the soup, and cook it for 10 minutes more.

per serving: 122 calories, 5.4g protein, 21g carbohydrates, 2.1g fat, 2.6g fiber, 0mg cholesterol, 139mg sodium, 323mg potassium.

Basil Soup

Yield: 4 servings | **Prep time:** 5 minutes
Cook time: 25 minutes

Ingredients:

- 1 cup white cabbage, shredded
- 1-pound chicken breast, skinless, boneless, chopped
- 1 tablespoon tomato paste
- ½ cup broccoli, shredded
- 1 tablespoon cream cheese
- 1 oz fresh basil, chopped

Directions:

1. Put all ingredients in the saucepan and close the lid.
2. Simmer the soup for 25 minutes over medium-low heat.

per serving: 144 calories, 24.8g protein, 2.8g carbohydrates, 3.2g fat, 1g fiber, 73mg cholesterol, 71mg sodium, 538mg potassium.

Chicken Chowder

Yield: 2 servings | **Prep time:** 5 minutes
Cook time: 20 minutes

Ingredients:

- ½ cup chicken fillet, diced
- ¼ cup leek, chopped
- 1 teaspoon dried cilantro
- 1 cup of water
- 1 cup plain yogurt
- 1 teaspoon olive oil

Directions:

1. Roast the diced chicken with olive oil in the pan for 10 minutes. Stir well.
2. Then add all remaining ingredients and close the lid.
3. Cook the chowder for 10 minutes more on medium heat.

per serving: 277 calories, 29.8g protein, 10.6g carbohydrates, 13g fat, 0.5g fiber, 92mg cholesterol, 180mg sodium, 536mg potassium.

SALADS

Salads

Chickpea Salad

Yield: 6 servings | **Prep time:** 10 minutes
Cook time: 0 minutes

Ingredients:

- 2 cups chickpeas, boiled
- 1 tablespoon olive oil
- ¼ teaspoon chili powder
- 1 avocado, pitted, peeled, and chopped
- ½ teaspoon lemon juice
- 1 oz parmesan, chopped

Directions:

1. Put all ingredients in the salad bowl and stir well.

per serving: 311 calories, 14.7g protein, 43.2g carbohydrates, 10.1g fat, 13.7g fiber, 3mg cholesterol, 61mg sodium, 746mg potassium.

Cheddar Cheese Salad

Yield: 4 servings | **Prep time:** 10 minutes
Cook time: 0 minutes

Ingredients:

- 2 tablespoons orange juice
- 2 oranges, chopped
- ¼ cup olive oil
- 2 cups romaine lettuce, chopped
- 1 apple, chopped
- 1 cup Cheddar cheese, shredded
- 1 red onion, diced

Directions:

1. Put all ingredients in the salad bowl and shake well.

per serving: 210 calories, 3.5g protein, 20.6g carbohydrates, 14.1g fat, 4.1g fiber, 4mg cholesterol, 46mg sodium, 301mg potassium.

Greece Style Salad

Yield: 4 servings | **Prep time:** 10 minutes
Cook time: 5 minutes

Ingredients:

- 2 cups lettuce, chopped
- 3 oz halloumi, roughly chopped
- 1 tablespoon olive oil
- 1 teaspoon avocado oil
- ½ cup cherry tomatoes, halved
- 1 tablespoon apple cider vinegar

Directions:

1. Sprinkle the halloumi cheese with olive oil and grill at 400F for 1 minute per side.

2. Then mix all ingredients in the salad bowl and shake well.

per serving: 95 calories, 3.9g protein, 1.8g carbohydrates 8.4g fat, 0.5g fiber, 0mg cholesterol, 5mg sodium, 95mg potassium.

Raisins Salad

Yield: 4 servings | **Prep time:** 10 minutes
Cook time: 0 minutes

Ingredients:

- 2 tablespoons avocado oil
- ½ cup raisins
- 4 tablespoons lemon juice
- 2 oz chives, chopped
- ½ cup cilantro, chopped
- ½ cup fresh dill, chopped
- 1 cup endives, chopped
- 1 cup radish, sliced
- ¼ teaspoon salt
- 1 tablespoon hemp seeds

Directions:

1. Put all ingredients in the salad bowl.
2. Stir the salad with the help of two spoons.

per serving: 109 calories, 3.2g protein, 21.9g carbohydrates, 2.6g fat, 3.6g fiber, 0mg cholesterol 186mg sodium, 573mg potassium.

Pesto Sauce Salad

Yield: 4 servings | **Prep time:** 10 minutes
Cook time: 10 minutes

Ingredients:

- 2 tomatoes, roughly chopped
- 1 ½ red onion, peeled, sliced
- 2 tablespoons avocado oil
- ½ teaspoon pesto sauce
- 8 oz chicken fillet, chopped
- 1 teaspoon lime juice

Directions:

1. Sprinkle the chicken fillet with lime juice and pesto sauce and grill it for 10 minutes at 400F (for 5 minutes per side). The chicken should be crunchy.
2. Then mix chicken with all remaining ingredients.

per serving: 196 calories,17.4g protein, 6.3g carbohydrates, 11.4g fat, 1.6g fiber, 50mg cholesterol 54mg sodium, 345mg potassium.

Beef Salad

Yield: 6 servings | **Prep time:** 10 minutes
Cook time: 15 minutes

Ingredients:

- 1-pound beef steak
- 1 teaspoon dried oregano
- 1 teaspoon dried rosemary
- 1 tablespoon olive oil
- 2 cups spinach, chopped
- 1 cup lettuce, chopped
- 1 tablespoon avocado oil

Directions:

1. Sprinkle the beef steak with dried oregano, dried rosemary, and olive oil.
2. Grill the steak for 7.5 minutes per side at 400F.
3. Then slice the meat and put it in the salad bowl.
4. Add all remaining ingredients and gently shake the salad.

per serving: 188 calories, 23.3g protein, 0.9g carbohydrates, 9.7g fat, 0.4g fiber, 68mg cholesterol, 59mg sodium, 379mg potassium.

Yogurt Salad

Yield: 6 servings | **Prep time:** 10 minutes
Cook time: 0 minutes

Ingredients:

- 3 cups spinach, chopped
- 2 sweet potatoes, peeled, cooked, chopped
- ½ cup Mozzarella cheese, shredded
- ¼ cup plain yogurt
- 1 teaspoon ground black pepper

Directions:

1. Mix the spinach and sweet potato in the salad bowl.
2. Add cheese and yogurt.
3. Then sprinkle the salad with ground black pepper and stir the salad well.

per serving: 50 calories, 3.1g protein, 2g carbohydrates, 3.3g fat, 0.3g fiber, 11mg cholesterol, 67mg sodium, 79mg potassium.

Goat Cheese Salad

Yield: 4 servings | **Prep time:** 10 minutes
Cook time: 0 minutes

Ingredients:

- 2 tablespoons olive oil
- 1 tablespoon lemon juice
- ½ teaspoon dried basil
- 1 cup cucumbers, chopped
- 2 oz Goat cheese, crumbled
- ¼ teaspoon chili flakes

Directions:

1. Put cucumbers in the salad bowl.
2. Add olive oil, lemon juice, basil, and chili flakes.
3. Stir the salad and top with crumbled Goat cheese.

per serving: 102 calories, 2.2g protein, 1.6g carbohydrates, 9.9g fat, 0.1g fiber, 13mg cholesterol, 159mg sodium, 50mg potassium.

Salad Mix

Yield: 4 servings | **Prep time:** 10 minutes
Cook time: 0 minutes

Ingredients:

- 1 cup red cabbage, shredded
- 1 cup white cabbage, shredded
- ½ cup carrot, peeled, grated
- ½ cup plain yogurt
- ¼ teaspoon salt
- ¼ teaspoon dried mint

Directions:

1. Mix red cabbage and white cabbage in the salad bowl.
2. Add carrot, salt, dried mint, and plain yogurt.
3. Carefully stir the salad.

per serving: 41 calories, 2.1g protein, 7.1g carbohydrates, 0.4g fat, 1.2g fiber, 2mg cholesterol, 173mg sodium, 134mg potassium.

Prune Salad

Yield: 4 servings | **Prep time:** 10 minutes
Cook time: 0 minutes

Ingredients:

- 7 oz fennel bulb, peeled, grated
- 2 oz raisins
- 3 tablespoons olive oil
- 1 teaspoon liquid honey
- ¼ teaspoon ground cinnamon
- 2 prunes, chopped

Directions:

1. Put all ingredients in the salad bowl and stir carefully.

per serving: 137 calories, 1.5g protein, 34.6g carbohydrates, 0.7g fat, 3.7g fiber, 2mg cholesterol, 43mg sodium, 471mg potassium.

Almond Salad with Fennel

Yield: 4 servings | **Prep time:** 5 minutes
Cook time: 0 minutes

Ingredients:

- 2 oz almonds, chopped
- 1 tablespoon lemon juice
- 8 oz fennel bulb, chopped
- ¼ teaspoon ground turmeric
- 1 tablespoon avocado oil

Directions:

1. Mix up all ingredients in the salad bowl.

per serving: 121 calories, 2.3g protein, 6.5g carbohydrates, 10.6g fat, 3.4g fiber, 0mg cholesterol, 30mg sodium, 310mg potassium.

Mustard Salad

Yield: 4 servings | **Prep time:** 7 minutes
Cook time: 0 minutes

Ingredients:

- 2 oz lettuce, chopped
- 2 tablespoons avocado oil
- ¼ teaspoon dried basil
- 1 teaspoon mustard
- 5 cups arugula, chopped
- 6 oz chicken, chopped, cooked

Directions:

1. Put all ingredients in the salad bowl and shake until you get a homogenous salad.

per serving: 84 calories, 13.3g protein, 1.7g carbohydrates, 2.6g fat, 0.9g fiber, 33mg cholesterol, 34mg sodium, 201mg potassium.

Watermelon Salad

Yield: 4 servings | **Prep time:** 5 minutes
Cook time: 0 minutes

Ingredients:

- 2 tomatoes, chopped
- 1 cup watermelon, chopped
- 2 tablespoons fresh parsley, chopped
- 1 tablespoon lemon juice
- 1 teaspoon olive oil

Directions:

1. Put all ingredients from the list above in the salad bowl and shake well.

per serving: 39 calories, 1.2g protein, 6.5g carbohydrates, 1.5g fat, 1.3g fiber, 0mg cholesterol, 13mg sodium, 306mg potassium.

Blackberries Salad

Yield: 4 servings | **Prep time:** 5 minutes
Cook time: 0 minutes

Ingredients:

- 1 cup blackberries
- 1 apple, chopped
- 2 bananas, chopped
- 1 tablespoon liquid honey
- 1 tablespoon cream cheese
- ½ teaspoon vanilla extract

Directions:

1. Put all ingredients in the salad bowl and stir well with the help of a spoon.

per serving: 100 calories, 1.3g protein, 24.4g carbohydrates, 0.7g fat, 4.1g fiber, 1mg cholesterol, 3mg sodium, 322mg potassium.

Quinoa Salad with Artichoke

Yield: 4 servings | **Prep time:** 8 minutes
Cook time: 0 minutes

Ingredients:

- 1/3 cup quinoa, cooked
- 3 artichoke hearts, chopped, canned
- 1 tablespoon avocado oil
- ½ teaspoon garlic, diced
- 1 tablespoon lemon juice
- ½ cup green olives, sliced

Directions:

1. In the bowl mix quinoa and artichoke hearts.
2. Then add garlic, green olive, and lemon juice.
3. Add avocado oil and stir the salad well.

per serving: 179 calories, 6.7g protein, 28.7g carbohydrates, 5.1g fat, 7.7g fiber, 0mg cholesterol, 357mg sodium, 536mg potassium.

Tender Chicken and Vegetables Salad

Yield: 4 servings | **Prep time:** 10 minutes
Cook time: 15 minutes

Ingredients:

- 4 slices of chicken fillet, chopped, cooked
- ½ teaspoon olive oil
- ¼ teaspoon ground black pepper
- 1-pound asparagus, trimmed
- 1 teaspoon sesame seeds
- 1 oz Cheddar cheese, grated

Directions:

1. Sprinkle asparagus with olive oil and ground black pepper and transfer to the lined baking tray.

2. Bake the vegetables for 15 minutes at 365F.
3. Then chop the asparagus roughly and put it in the salad bowl.
4. Add chicken, sesame seeds, olive oil, and Cheddar cheese.
5. Shake the salad gently.

per serving: 99 calories, 10.7g protein, 4.8g carbohydrates, 4.6g fat, 2.5g fiber, 24mg cholesterol, 35mg sodium, 298mg potassium.

Apple Salad

Yield: 4 servings | **Prep time:** 10 minutes
Cook time: 0 minutes

Ingredients:

- 2 cup lettuce, chopped
- 1 apple, chopped
- ½ cup tomatoes, chopped
- 2 tablespoons balsamic vinegar
- 3 oz Mozzarella, chopped
- 1 teaspoon olive oil

Directions:

1. In the bowl combine lettuce, apple, tomatoes, and Mozzarella.
2. Add balsamic vinegar and olive oil.
3. Stir the salad.

per serving: 98 calories, 6.6g protein, 7.4g carbohydrates, 5.1g fat, 1.5g fiber, 11mg cholesterol, 132mg sodium, 136mg potassium.

Onion Salad

Yield: 4 servings | **Prep time:** 5 minutes
Cook time: 0 minutes

Ingredients:

- 1 cup quinoa, cooked
- ½ cup lettuce, chopped
- 1 red onion, sliced
- 2 tablespoons lemon juice
- 1 tablespoon avocado oil
- ¼ cup green peas, cooked

Directions:

1. Put all ingredients in the mixing bowl.
2. Stir the salad until homogenous.

per serving: 200 calories, 10.1g protein, 33.9g carbohydrates, 3.6g fat, 9.5g fiber, 0mg cholesterol, 16mg sodium, 509mg potassium.

Feta and Herbs Salad

Yield: 3 servings | **Prep time:** 5 minutes
Cook time: 0 minutes

Ingredients:

- 1 tablespoon Italian seasonings
- 4 oz Feta, chopped
- 1 red onion, sliced
- 1 tablespoon olive oil
- 1 teaspoon dried thyme

Directions:

1. Put all ingredients in the bowl and stir.

per serving: 164 calories, 5.8g protein, 5.5g carbohydrates, 13.5g fat, 0.8g fiber, 35mg cholesterol, 511mg sodium, 78mg potassium.

Fine Bulgur and Tomato Salad

Yield: 6 servings | **Prep time:** 10 minutes
Cook time: 0 minutes

Ingredients:

- 1 cup tomatoes, finely chopped
- ½ cup bulgur, cooked
- 2 tablespoons dried basil
- ¼ cup plain yogurt
- 1 teaspoon tomato paste

Directions:

1. Put all ingredients in the salad bowl.
2. Stir the salad well with the help of the spoon.

per serving: 60 calories, 2.2g protein, 12.9g carbohydrates, 0.3g fat, 2.5g fiber, 1mg cholesterol, 10mg sodium, 120mg potassium.

Fish Salad

Yield: 8 servings | **Prep time:** 10 minutes
Cook time: 0 minutes

Ingredients:

- 1 cup corn kernels, cooked
- 9 oz salmon, boiled
- ½ cup fresh dill, chopped
- ¼ cup plain yogurt

Directions:

1. Mix up corn kernels, salmon, fresh dill, and yogurt in the bowl.
2. Stir the salad until homogenous.

per serving: 83 calories, 9.6g protein, 4.4g carbohydrates, 2.9g fat, 0.7g fiber, 10mg cholesterol, 26mg sodium, 197mg potassium.

Orange Salad

Yield: 2 servings | **Prep time:** 5 minutes
Cook time: 0 minutes

Ingredients:

- 1 orange, peeled and chopped
- ¼ cup walnuts, chopped
- 1 cup lettuce, chopped
- 1 tablespoon olive oil
- 4 oz Parmesan, chopped

Directions:

1. Put all ingredients from the list above in the salad bowl.
2. Shake the salad gently.

per serving: 196 calories,5.5g protein, 9.3g carbohydrates, 16.7g fat, 2.6g fiber, 0mg cholesterol, 5mg sodium, 263mg potassium.

Red Salad

Yield: 4 servings | **Prep time:** 10 minutes
Cook time: 0 minutes

Ingredients:

- 2 cups tomatoes, roughly chopped
- 1 tablespoon Dijon mustard
- 1 teaspoon olive oil
- 1 teaspoon apple cider vinegar
- 5 oz Feta cheese, crumbled

Directions:

1. In the shallow bowl, mix Dijon mustard, olive oil, and apple cider vinegar.
2. Then place all remaining ingredients in the salad bowl and top with Dijon mustard mixture.

per serving: 194 calories,21.5g protein, 12.1g carbohydrates, 6.6g fat, 1g fiber, 63mg cholesterol, 112mg sodium, 344mg potassium.

Tilapia Salad

Yield: 6 servings | **Prep time:** 10 minutes
Cook time: 4 minutes

Ingredients:

- 1-pound tilapia fillet
- 1 teaspoon Italian seasonings
- 2 cups lettuce, chopped
- 1 tablespoon lemon juice
- 2 tablespoons Plain yogurt
- ½ teaspoon salt

Directions:

1. Sprinkle the tilapia fillet with Italian seasonings and salt.

2. Grill the fish at 400F for 2 minutes per side.
3. Then roughly chop the fish and put it in the salad bowl.
4. Add lettuce, lemon juice, and Plain yogurt.
5. Stir the salad well.

per serving: 109 calories,15g protein, 1g carbohydrates, 5g fat, 0.1g fiber, 34mg cholesterol, 232mg sodium, 330mg potassium.

Ginger Salad with Yogurt

Yield: 4 servings | **Prep time:** 10 minutes
Cook time: 0 minutes

Ingredients:

- 1 cup celery stalk, chopped
- ¼ cup Plain yogurt
- 1 cucumber, chopped
- 1 oz fresh ginger, peeled, grated
- 1 cup lettuce, chopped

Directions:

1. Mix celery stalk and cucumber.
2. Then add yogurt and all remaining ingredients.
3. Stir the salad.

per serving: 28 calories, 1.6g protein, 5g carbohydrates, 0.4g fat, 0.9g fiber, 1mg cholesterol, 33mg sodium, 223mg potassium.

Sweet Salad

Yield: 4 servings | **Prep time:** 7 minutes
Cook time: 0 minutes

Ingredients:

- 1 cup mango, chopped
- 1 cup lettuce, chopped
- ¼ cup mozzarella, shredded
- 3 tablespoons olive oil

Directions:

1. Mix all ingredients in the salad bowl.

per serving: 37 calories, 1g protein, 6.7g carbohydrates, 1g fat, 0.7g fiber, 3mg cholesterol, 15mg sodium, 91mg potassium.

Easy Caesar

Yield: 4 servings | **Prep time:** 10 minutes
Cook time: 0 minutes

Ingredients:

- 1 cup lettuce, chopped
- 3 oz Parmesan, grated
- 5 oz chicken fillet, cooked, shredded
- 4 tablespoons Plain yogurt
- 1 teaspoon walnuts, chopped

- 1 cup arugula, chopped

Directions:

1. Put lettuce and chicken in the salad bowl.
2. Then add plain yogurt, walnuts, and arugula, and shake the salad one more time.
3. Top the cooked Caesar with Parmesan.

per serving: 152 calories, 18.2g protein, 3.1g carbohydrates, 7.5g fat, 0.4g fiber, 48mg cholesterol, 240mg sodium, 195mg potassium.

Meat Salad

Yield: 6 servings | Prep time: 10 minutes
Cook time: 10 minutes

Ingredients:

- 2 cups lettuce, chopped
- 1 cup ground pork
- 1 teaspoon onion powder
- 1 tablespoon olive oil
- ¼ cup parmesan cheese, shredded
- 1 tablespoon olive oil
- 1 teaspoon mustard

Directions:

1. Mix ground pork and onion powder.
2. Make the meatballs from the meat mixture.
3. Then toss olive oil in the saucepan and melt it.
4. Add meatballs and cook them for 4 minutes per side on medium-low heat.
5. Then transfer the meatballs to the salad bowl.
6. Add lettuce and cheese. Shake the salad gently.
7. Then sprinkle it with olive oil and mustard.

per serving: 145 calories, 16.1g protein, 1.1g carbohydrates, 8.3g fat, 0.6g fiber, 45mg cholesterol, 65mg sodium, 298mg potassium.

Beans Salad

Yield: 4 servings | Prep time: 7 minutes
Cook time: 0 minutes

Ingredients:

- 1 cup white beans, boiled
- ¼ cup quinoa, cooked
- 4 tablespoons plain yogurt
- 3 oz red onion, chopped
- 1 teaspoon chili flakes

Directions:

1. Put all ingredients in the salad bowl and stir well.

per serving: 75 calories, 4g protein, 10.6g carbohydrates, 1.6g fiber, 1.8g fiber, 1mg cholesterol, 83mg sodium, 152mg potassium.

Grape Salad

Yield: 4 servings | Prep time: 0 minutes
Cook time: 0 minutes

Ingredients:

- 8 oz celeriac root, grated
- 3 oz green grapes, halved
- 1 apple, grated
- 1 tablespoon ground cinnamon
- 2 tablespoons lemon juice

Directions:

1. Mix all remaining ingredients, and stir the salad.

per serving: 76 calories, 0.5g protein, 19.9g carbohydrates, 0.2g fat, 2.7g fiber, 0mg cholesterol, 62mg sodium, 125mg potassium.

Pomegranate Salad

Yield: 4 servings | Prep time: 8 minutes
Cook time: 0 minutes

Ingredients:

- ½ cup pomegranate seeds
- 3 oz Parmesan, shaved
- 1 cup arugula, chopped
- 2 tablespoons avocado oil

Directions:

1. Put arugula and pomegranate seeds in the salad bowl.
2. Add avocado oil and stir well.
3. Then top the salad with shaved Parmesan.

per serving: 143 calories, 7g protein, 4.2g carbohydrates, 11.6g fat, 0.2g fiber, 15mg cholesterol, 198mg sodium, 19mg potassium.

Banana Salad

Yield: 4 servings | Prep time: 5 minutes
Cook time: 0 minutes

Ingredients:

- 2 bananas, peeled, roughly chopped
- 2 pecans, chopped
- 2 tablespoons Plain yogurt
- 1 tablespoon raisins
- ¼ teaspoon lemon juice

Directions:

1. Mix bananas with pecans in the bowl.
2. Add raisins and lemon juice. Shake the salad.
3. Then add yogurt and stir it well.

per serving: 159 calories, 4.3g protein, 19.3g carbohydrates, 8.7g fat, 3.9g fiber, 0mg cholesterol, 7mg sodium, 235mg potassium.

Layer's Salad

Yield: 6 servings | **Prep time:** 10 minutes
Cook time: 0 minutes

Ingredients:

- 5 tomatoes
- 2 teaspoons fresh cilantro
- 2 tablespoons avocado oil
- ¼ teaspoon ground black pepper
- 3 oz Mozzarella, sliced

Directions:

1. Slice the tomatoes and place them on the plate in one layer.
2. Add sliced Mozzarella.
3. Then sprinkle the salad with fresh cilantro, avocado oil, and ground black pepper.

per serving: 99 calories, 4.9g protein, 4.6g carbohydrates, 7.4g fat, 1.3g fiber, 8mg cholesterol, 90mg sodium, 245mg potassium.

Heart of Palm and Feta Salad

Yield: 4 servings | **Prep time:** 10 minutes
Cook time: 0 minutes

Ingredients:

- 1 cup heart of palm, canned, chopped
- 1 cucumber, chopped
- 1 teaspoon lemon juice
- 1 oz Feta cheese, crumbled
- 1 tablespoon olive oil

Directions:

1. Put all ingredients from the list above in the salad bowl.
2. Stir them carefully with the help of a spoon.

per serving: 62 calories, 2.1g protein, 2.6g carbohydrates, 5.2g fat, 1.1g fiber, 6mg cholesterol, 235mg sodium, 107mg potassium.

Garlic and Eggplants Salad

Yield: 2 servings | **Prep time:** 15 minutes
Cook time: 5 minutes

Ingredients:

- 1 eggplant, trimmed
- 1 garlic clove, minced
- 1 tablespoon avocado oil
- 1 teaspoon olive oil
- ¼ cup fresh dill
- 1 tablespoon apple cider vinegar

Directions:

1. Chop the eggplant roughly and sprinkle it with olive oil.
2. Then cook the eggplant in the preheated to 400F grill for 1 minute per side.
3. Transfer the cooked eggplant to the salad bowl.
4. Sprinkle the eggplants with garlic.
5. Add all remaining ingredients, stir well, and leave the salad in the fridge for 10 minutes.

per serving: 142 calories, 2.4g protein, 14.1g carbohydrates, 9.7g fat, 8.2g fiber, 0mg cholesterol, 6mg sodium, 546mg potassium.

RICE
& GRAINS

Rice and Grains

Basil Basmati Rice

Yield: 5 servings | **Prep time:** 5 minutes
Cook time: 17 minutes

Ingredients:

- 1 cup basmati rice
- 1 tablespoon avocado oil
- 1 teaspoon dried basil
- 2 ½ cup water

Directions:

1. Heat the avocado oil in the saucepan.
2. Add rice and roast it for 2 minutes. Stir it constantly.
3. Then add basil and water.
4. Stir the rice and close the lid.
5. Cook it for 15 minutes or until it soaks all water.

per serving: 159 calories, 2.7g protein, 29.7g carbohydrates, 3g fat, 0.6g fiber, 0mg cholesterol, 6mg sodium, 46mg potassium.

Coconut Rice

Yield: 4 servings | **Prep time:** 5 minutes
Cook time: 20 minutes

Ingredients:

- ¼ cup basmati rice
- 1 cup coconut milk
- 2 oz dried cranberries
- ¼ teaspoon ground ginger

Directions:

1. Put all ingredients in the saucepan, stir, and close the lid.
2. Cook the rice on low heat for 20 minutes.

per serving: 65 calories, 1.1g protein, 12.6g carbohydrates, 0.7g fat, 0.7g fiber, 0mg cholesterol, 36mg sodium, 38mg potassium.

Feta Wild Rice

Yield: 5 servings | **Prep time:** 10 minutes
Cook time: 25 minutes

Ingredients:

- 1 cup wild rice
- 3 cups chicken stock
- 1 teaspoon dried thyme
- 2 oz Feta, crumbled
- 1 tablespoon avocado oil

Directions:

1. Mix wild rice with avocado oil and chicken stock.
2. Close the lid and cook it for 25 minutes over medium-low heat.
3. Then add dried thyme and crumbled feta.
4. Stir the rice.

per serving: 177 calories, 6.7g protein, 25g carbohydrates, 6.1g fat, 2g fiber, 11mg cholesterol, 587mg sodium, 153mg potassium.

Curry Brown Rice

Yield: 3 servings | **Prep time:** 5 minutes
Cook time: 20 minutes

Ingredients:

- 3 oz brown rice
- 9 oz chicken stock
- 1 teaspoon curry powder
- ½ teaspoon garlic, minced
- 4 tablespoons olive oil
- 1 tablespoon cream cheese

Directions:

1. Heat olive oil in the saucepan.
2. Add garlic.
3. Add brown rice, curry powder, and chicken stock.
4. Close the lid and saute the rice for 15 minutes.
5. Add cream cheese and stir the meal well.

per serving: 283 calories, 2.9g protein, 25.7g carbohydrates, 19.8g fat, 2g fiber, 0mg cholesterol, 269mg sodium, 145mg potassium.

Rice and Cheese Meatballs

Yield: 6 servings | **Prep time:** 10 minutes
Cook time: 25 minutes

Ingredients:

- ¼ cup Mozzarella cheese, shredded
- 1 teaspoon ground coriander
- 1 cup of basmati rice, cooked
- ¼ cup ground chicken
- 1 teaspoon olive oil

Directions:

1. In the mixing bowl, mix Mozzarella cheese, ground coriander, rice, and ground chicken.
2. Then make the balls from the mixture.
3. Heat the olive oil well and put the rice balls in the hot oil.
4. Roast the balls for 1 minute per side on high heat.
5. Then transfer the balls to the oven and bake them for 20 minutes at 360F.

per serving: 150 calories, 5.1g protein, 24.9g carbohydrates, 3g fat, 0.5g fiber, 10mg cholesterol, 36mg sodium, 59mg potassium.

Italian Style Rice

Yield: 4 servings | **Prep time:** 8 minutes
Cook time: 15 minutes

Ingredients:

- ½ cup of basmati rice
- 1.5 cups of water
- 2 tablespoons pesto sauce
- 1 teaspoon olive oil
- 1 teaspoon cream cheese

Directions:

1. Simmer the rice water for 15 minutes on low heat or until the rice soaks all liquid.
2. Then mix cooked rice with pesto sauce, olive oil, and cream cheese.

per serving: 118 calories, 2.4g protein, 19g carbohydrates, 3.4g fat, 0.4g fiber, 2mg cholesterol, 51mg sodium, 27mg potassium.

Rice Bowl

Yield: 4 servings | **Prep time:** 10 minutes
Cook time: 0 minutes

Ingredients:

- ½ cup long-grain rice, cooked
- ½ cup corn kernels, cooked
- 1 cucumber, chopped
- 1 teaspoon chili flakes
- ¼ cup plain yogurt
- 1 celery stalk, chopped

Directions:

1. Mix all ingredients with cooked rice.
2. Place the cooked meal into the bowl.

per serving: 117 calories, 3.4g protein, 24.2g carbohydrates, 0.6g fat, 1.2g fiber, 1mg cholesterol, 158mg sodium, 167mg potassium.

Turmeric Paella

Yield: 4 servings | **Prep time:** 10 minutes
Cook time: 30 minutes

Ingredients:

- 1 cup risotto rice
- 2 oz yellow onion, diced
- ½ teaspoon ground turmeric
- 1 cup sweet pepper, chopped
- 1 cup shrimp, peeled
- 1 teaspoon olive oil
- 3 cups of water

Directions:

1. Heat olive oil in the saucepan.

2. Add onion and cook it for 2 minutes.
3. Then stir well, add shrimp, ground turmeric, and sweet pepper, and stir well.
4. Cook the ingredients for 5 minutes.
5. Add water and risotto rice. Stir well, close the lid, and cook the meal for 20 minutes on low heat.

per serving: 208 calories, 7.4g protein, 40.5g carbohydrates, 1.6g fat, 1.5g fiber, 50mg cholesterol, 125mg sodium, 188mg potassium.

Chicken and Parsley Rice

Yield: 5 servings | **Prep time:** 10 minutes
Cook time: 20 minutes

Ingredients:

- 1 cup basmati rice
- 3 tablespoons avocado oil
- 2.5 cups water
- ½ teaspoon dried parsley
- 10 oz chicken breast, skinless, boneless, chopped

Directions:

1. Mix oil with rice and roast it in the saucepan for 5 minutes over low heat.
2. Then add chicken and water.
3. Add parsley, stir the ingredients, and cook the meal on medium heat for 15 minutes or until all ingredients are cooked.

per serving: 216 calories, 15.1g protein, 30.5g carbohydrates, 3g fat, 0.9g fiber, 36mg cholesterol, 413mg sodium, 290mg potassium.

Chives and Jasmine Rice

Yield: 4 servings | **Prep time:** 10 minutes
Cook time: 10 minutes

Ingredients:

- 3 tablespoons olive oil
- 1 cup jasmine rice
- 2 tablespoons chives, chopped
- ½ teaspoon ground black pepper
- 2 teaspoons lime juice

Directions:

1. Cook the rice according to the directions of the manufacturer.
2. Then add chives, olive oil, ground black pepper, and lime juice.
3. Carefully stir the meal.

per serving: 250 calories, 3.1g protein, 36.4g carbohydrates, 10.2g fat, 2.2g fiber, 0mg cholesterol, 1mg sodium, 15mg potassium.

Carrot Jambalaya

Yield: 8 servings | **Prep time:** 5 minutes
Cook time: 30 minutes

Ingredients:

- 1 cup tomatoes, chopped
- 1 cup bell pepper, chopped
- ¼ cup carrot, chopped
- 1 teaspoon cayenne pepper
- 4 cups water
- 1 cup of basmati rice
- 2 tablespoons avocado oil
- ½ cup chickpeas, cooked

Directions:

1. Melt the avocado oil and add carrot, bell pepper, and tomatoes.
2. Cook the vegetables for 10 minutes on medium heat.
3. Then add water, chickpeas, and rice
4. Add cayenne pepper and stir the meal.
5. Close the lid and cook it for 20 minutes on low heat.

per serving: 175 calories, 4.8g protein, 28.9g carbohydrates, 4.7g fat, 3.1g fiber, 0mg cholesterol, 390mg sodium, 240mg potassium.

Zucchini and Rice

Yield: 4 servings | **Prep time:** 10 minutes
Cook time: 20 minutes

Ingredients:

- 1 cup basmati rice
- 3 cups chicken stock
- 1 teaspoon ground cumin
- ¼ teaspoon dried thyme
- 2 tablespoons olive oil
- 1 zucchini, grated

Directions:

1. Roast the rice with olive oil in the saucepan for 5 minutes. Stir it.
2. Then add thyme, cumin, and grated zucchini.
3. Add water, mix the rice mixture, and close the lid.
4. Cook the rice for 15 minutes over medium heat.

per serving: 153 calories, 2.9g protein, 19.6g carbohydrates, 7.3g fat, 1.4g fiber, 0mg cholesterol, 581mg sodium, 93mg potassium.

Vegetable Pilaf

Yield: 4 servings | **Prep time:** 10 minutes
Cook time: 25 minutes

Ingredients:

- 2 cups of water
- ½ cup white onion, diced
- 1 cup white mushrooms, chopped
- 1 cup of basmati rice
- 2 oz feta cheese, crumbled
- 2 tablespoons olive oil

Directions:

1. Put rice in the saucepan.
2. Add water and cook for 15 minutes over low heat.
3. Then roast the mushrooms with olive oil and white onion in the skillet until they are light brown.
4. Add the cooked mushrooms to the cooked rice. Stir well.
5. Top the meal with crumbled Feta cheese.

per serving: 304 calories, 8.2g protein, 39.4g carbohydrates, 12.4g fat, 1g fiber, 15mg cholesterol, 57mg sodium, 163mg potassium.

Celery Rice

Yield: 4 servings | **Prep time:** 10 minutes
Cook time: 30 minutes

Ingredients:

- 2 cups wild rice
- 1 teaspoon Italian seasonings
- 1 tablespoon olive oil
- ¼ cup onion, diced
- ½ cup celery stalk, chopped
- 5 cups of water

Directions:

1. Mix 4 cups of water and wild rice in the saucepan.
2. Cook the rice for 15 minutes or until the rice soaks all liquid.
3. Then heat the olive oil in the separated saucepan.
4. Add onion and roast it until light brown.
5. Add celery stalk, water, and rice.
6. Stir well and close the lid.
7. Cook the rice for 10 minutes.

per serving: 337 calories, 12.8g protein, 63.4g carbohydrates, 4.7g fat, 6.1g fiber, 1mg cholesterol, 21mg sodium, 411mg potassium.

Grilled Pears and Rice

Yield: 5 servings | **Prep time:** 10 minutes
Cook time: 20 minutes

Ingredients:

- 1 cup of basmati rice
- 2.5 cups chicken stock
- 1 teaspoon olive oil
- 1 pear, halved

Directions:

1. Sprinkle the pears with olive oil and grill in the

preheated to 400F grill for 1 minute per side. Chop the cooked pears roughly.
2. Then cook rice with chicken stock for 15 minutes.
3. Transfer the cooked rice to the bowls and top with grilled pears.

per serving: 157 calories, 3.4g protein, 31.9g carbohydrates, 1.6g fat, 1.1g fiber, 0mg cholesterol, 386mg sodium, 166mg potassium.

Beef and Rice Bowl

Yield: 6 servings | Prep time: 10 minutes
Cook time: 0 minutes

Ingredients:

- 1 cup purple cabbage, shredded
- 1 cup long grain rice, cooked
- 8 oz beef steak, cooked, cut into the strips
- 1/3 cup plain yogurt
- 1 teaspoon salt
- 1 teaspoon dried rosemary

Directions:

1. Put cabbage and rice in the big bowl.
2. Add white rice and meat strips.
3. Then add plain yogurt, rosemary, and salt.
4. Stir the mixture until homogenous.

per serving: 195 calories, 14.6g protein, 26.3g carbohydrates, 2.7g fat, 0.7g fiber, 35mg cholesterol, 426mg sodium, 240mg potassium.

Rice with Apricots

Yield: 7 servings | Prep time: 5 minutes
Cook time: 20 minutes

Ingredients:

- 1.5 cups basmati rice
- 3 tablespoons olive oil
- 5 apricots, pitted, chopped
- ¼ cup cream cheese
- 3.5 cups water
- ½ teaspoon salt

Directions:

1. Mix water and basmati rice in the saucepan and boil for 15 minutes on low heat.
2. Then add cream cheese, salt, and apricots.
3. Stir the rice carefully and bring it to a boil.
4. Add olive oil and cook for 1 minute more.

per serving: 290 calories, 3.7g protein, 55g carbohydrates, 5.9g fat, 3.1g fiber, 2mg cholesterol, 176mg sodium, 313mg potassium.

Tomatoes Rice

Yield: 4 servings | Prep time: 10 minutes
Cook time: 0 minutes

Ingredients:

- 1 cup of basmati rice, cooked
- 4 oz beef sirloin, grilled
- ½ cup tomatoes, chopped
- 2 tablespoons apple cider vinegar
- 1 teaspoon ground coriander
- 2 oz scallions, sliced

Directions:

1. Put the cooked rice in the serving bowls.
2. Add beef sirloin, tomatoes, and scallions.
3. Then sprinkle the meal with apple cider vinegar and ground coriander.

per serving: 236 calories, 12.9g protein, 39.8g carbohydrates, 2.2g fat, 1.5g fiber, 25mg cholesterol, 475mg sodium, 290mg potassium.

Eggplant and Rice

Yield: 2 servings | Prep time: 10 minutes
Cook time: 25 minutes

Ingredients:

- ½ cup of long-grain rice
- 1.5 cup chicken stock
- 1 eggplant, peeled, cubed
- 1 tablespoon olive oil
- 1 teaspoon ground paprika
- 1 tablespoon raisins

Directions:

1. Mix rice and chicken stock in the saucepan and cook for 15 minutes or until the rice soaks the liquid.
2. Then heat the olive oil.
3. Add eggplant to the oil and roast for 5 minutes.
4. After this, sprinkle the eggplant with ground paprika, and add raisins and rice.
5. Carefully mix the rice and cook for 5 minutes.

per serving: 269 calories, 5.3g protein, 45g carbohydrates, 8.1g fat, 2.2g fiber, 0mg cholesterol, 586mg sodium, 370mg potassium.

Rice Cakes

Yield: 4 servings | Prep time: 10 minutes
Cook time: 10 minutes

Ingredients:

- 6 oz tilapia fillet, boiled, chopped
- 1 egg, beaten
- ¼ cup of basmati rice, cooked

- 1 teaspoon dried parsley
- ½ teaspoon ground black pepper
- 1 tablespoon olive oil

Directions:

1. Mix tilapia with egg, basmati rice, dried parsley, and ground black pepper.
2. Heat the olive oil in the skillet.
3. Make the small cakes from the tilapia mixture and put them in the hot oil.
4. Roast the cakes for 2 minutes per side or until they are light brown.

per serving: 145 calories, 10.5g protein, 9.3g carbohydrates, 7.3g fat, 0.2g fiber, 60mg cholesterol, 35mg sodium, 192mg potassium.

Shrimp Rice

Yield: 4 servings | **Prep time:** 10 minutes
Cook time: 30 minutes

Ingredients:

- 6 oz shrimp, frozen
- ½ cup of long-grain rice
- 3 cups of water
- 1 tablespoon avocado oil
- ½ teaspoon smoked paprika

Directions:

1. Boil the rice with water for 15-18 minutes or until it soaks all water.
2. Then avocado olive oil in the saucepan.
3. Add shrimp and smoked paprika. Cook the ingredients for 10 minutes on low heat.
4. Then add rice, stir well, and cook for 5 minutes more.

per serving: 139 calories, 5.7g protein, 19.1g carbohydrates, 3.9g fat, 0.3g fiber, 29mg cholesterol, 94mg sodium, 29mg potassium.

Seafood and Rice Stew

Yield: 4 servings | **Prep time:** 10 minutes
Cook time: 30 minutes

Ingredients:

- 5 oz long-grain rice
- 4 oz squid, sliced
- 1 chili pepper, chopped
- ½ cup cherry tomatoes, chopped
- 1 onion, diced
- 2 cups water
- 1 tablespoon avocado oil

Directions:

1. Roast the onion with avocado oil in the skillet for 3-4 minutes or until the onion is light brown.

2. Add squid, chili pepper, and cherry tomatoes.
3. Cook the ingredients for 7 minutes.
4. Then cook rice with water for 15 minutes.
5. Add cooked rice to the squid mixture, stir, and cook for 3 minutes more.

per serving: 181 calories, 7.9g protein, 33.4g carbohydrates, 1.4g fat, 1.6g fiber, 66mg cholesterol, 398mg sodium, 230mg potassium.

Salsa and Pesto Rice

Yield: 6 servings | **Prep time:** 10 minutes
Cook time: 15 minutes

Ingredients:

- 9 oz long-grain rice
- 4 cups water
- 2 tablespoons pesto
- 1 cup of salsa
- 2 tablespoons avocado oil

Directions:

1. Mix water and rice in the saucepan.
2. Cook the rice for 15 minutes on medium heat.
3. Then cool it to room temperature and mix it with avocado oil, pesto, and salsa.

per serving: 180 calories, 4.2g protein, 37.5g carbohydrates, 1.3g fat, 1.4g fiber, 0mg cholesterol, 771mg sodium, 202mg potassium.

Mint and Chicken Pilaf

Yield: 4 servings | **Prep time:** 10 minutes
Cook time: 30 minutes

Ingredients:

- 1 cup of long-grain rice
- 2 cups of water
- 10 oz chicken fillet, chopped
- 2 tablespoons olive oil
- 1 tablespoon dried parsley
- ½ teaspoon dried mint
- ½ teaspoon salt

Directions:

1. Boil rice with water for 15 minutes on medium heat.
2. Meanwhile, preheat the olive oil and add the chicken.
3. Roast the chicken for 10 minutes or until it is soft.
4. Then add dried parsley, mint, and cooked rice.
5. Carefully stir the pilaf and cook for 5 minutes.

per serving: 236 calories, 3.6g protein, 38.9g carbohydrates, 7.1g fat, 1.1g fiber, 0mg cholesterol, 309mg sodium, 130mg potassium.

Cabbage Rolls

Yield: 4 servings | **Prep time:** 15 minutes
Cook time: 35 minutes

Ingredients:

- 4 white cabbage leaves
- 4 oz lean ground beef
- ½ teaspoon garlic, minced
- ¼ cup of long-grain rice, cooked
- ½ cup water
- ½ cup tomatoes, chopped

Directions:

1. In the bowl, mix ground beef, garlic, and rice.
2. Then put the rice mixture on every cabbage leaf and roll.
3. Arrange the rice rolls in the saucepan.
4. Add water and tomatoes and close the lid.
5. Cook the rice rolls for 35 minutes on low heat.

per serving: 106 calories, 9.6g protein, 11.3g carbohydrates, 2.3g fat, 0.8g fiber, 25mg cholesterol, 124mg sodium, 167mg potassium.

Coconut Milk Millet

Yield: 4 servings | **Prep time:** 10 minutes
Cook time: 10 minutes

Ingredients:

- ½ cup millet
- ¼ cup coconut milk
- ¼ teaspoon ground cinnamon
- 1.5 cups hot water

Directions:

1. Mix hot water and millet in the saucepan.
2. Boil it for 8 minutes on low heat.
3. Add coconut milk and ground cinnamon.
4. Carefully stir the cooked millet.

per serving: 113 calories, 3g protein, 19.1g carbohydrates, 2.6g fat, 2.1g fiber, 5mg cholesterol, 160mg sodium, 60mg potassium.

Oatmeal and Zucchini Cakes

Yield: 4 servings | **Prep time:** 15 minutes
Cook time: 7 minutes

Ingredients:

- ½ cup oatmeal
- 1 egg, beaten
- 1 zucchini, grated
- 1 tablespoon avocado oil
- 1 teaspoon flax meal

Directions:

1. Put oatmeal, egg, grated zucchini, and flax meal in the blender. Blend the mixture well.
2. Then heat avocado oil in the skillet.
3. Make the medium size cakes from the oatmeal mixture and cook for 3 minutes per side on medium heat.

per serving: 93 calories, 3g protein, 8.7g carbohydrates, 5.5g fat, 1.6g fiber, 41mg cholesterol, 27mg sodium, 105mg potassium.

Cream Cheese Buckwheat

Yield: 2 servings | **Prep time:** 5 minutes
Cook time: 13 minutes

Ingredients:

- ½ cup buckwheat
- 1.5 cup water
- 3 oz cream cheese

Directions:

1. Put all ingredients in the saucepan and close the lid.
2. Cook the meal for 13 minutes on low heat or until the buckwheat soaks all liquid.
3. Carefully stir the cooked meal.

per serving: 159 calories, 6.6g protein, 31.5g carbohydrates, 2g fat, 4.3g fiber, 0mg cholesterol, 579mg sodium, 224mg potassium.

Cheesy Buckwheat

Yield: 4 servings | **Prep time:** 10 minutes
Cook time: 15 minutes

Ingredients:

- 1 cup buckwheat
- 2.5 cups water
- 4 oz Mozzarella, shredded
- 1 tablespoon olive oil
- ½ teaspoon dried oregano

Directions:

1. Mix water and buckwheat in the saucepan, bring to a boil, and cook for 7 minutes on medium heat.
2. After this, sprinkle Mozzarella cheese with olive oil and dried oregano.
3. Grill it for 2 minutes per side or until the cheese is light brown.
4. Then put the cooked buckwheat in the bowls.
5. Chop the cheese roughly and top the buckwheat with it.

per serving: 287 calories, 12.2g protein, 31.7g carbohydrates, 13.9g fat, 4.3g fiber, 23mg cholesterol, 625mg sodium, 252mg potassium.

Pesto Millet

Yield: 5 servings | **Prep time:** 10 minutes
Cook time: 7 minutes

Ingredients:

- 1 cup millet
- 2 cups chicken stock
- 4 tablespoons pesto sauce
- ¼ teaspoon dried dill

Directions:

1. Mix chicken stock and millet in the saucepan and boil for 7 minutes.
2. Then add dried dill and pesto sauce.
3. Stir the millet until homogenous and green.

per serving: 205 calories, 5.6g protein, 30g carbohydrates, 6.9g fat, 3.6g fiber, 3mg cholesterol, 81mg sodium, 81mg potassium.

Honey Quinoa

Yield: 4 servings | **Prep time:** 5 minutes
Cook time: 20 minutes

Ingredients:

- ½ cup butternut squash, peeled, cubed
- 1 tablespoon lime juice
- 1 teaspoon liquid honey
- 1 cup quinoa
- 2 cups of water
- ¼ cup coconut milk

Directions:

1. Put coconut milk and butternut squash in the saucepan.
2. Add lime juice and water.
3. Cook the butternut squash for 10 minutes.
4. Then add quinoa and cook the meal for 10 minutes.
5. Remove the cooked meal from the heat, add liquid honey, and stir well.

per serving: 177 calories, 6.4g protein, 31.8g carbohydrates, 2.9g fat, 3.9g fiber, 0mg cholesterol, 17mg sodium, 309mg potassium.

Tender Quinoa

Yield: 4 servings | **Prep time:** 5 minutes
Cook time: 4 minutes

Ingredients:

- 1 cup quinoa
- 2 cups of water
- 1 cup organic almond milk
- 3 oz almond flakes
- ¼ teaspoon ground cinnamon

Directions:

1. Pour water and almond milk into the saucepan and bring to a boil.
2. Add quinoa and cook it for 12 minutes.
3. Then cool the cooked quinoa and add honey and ground cinnamon.
4. Transfer the quinoa to the bowls and top with almond flakes.

per serving: 193 calories, 6.4g protein, 35g carbohydrates, 3.3g fat, 3.4g fiber, 0mg cholesterol, 41mg sodium, 271mg potassium.

Kale Rolls

Yield: 8 servings | **Prep time:** 10 minutes
Cook time: 1 minute

Ingredients:

- 8 rice pepper wraps
  1 cup quinoa, cooked
- 1 carrot, cut into strips
- 8 kale leaves
- 1 tablespoon avocado oil
- ½ teaspoon sesame seeds

Directions:

1. Make the rice pepper wraps wet.
2. Then put the cooked quinoa on every rice pepper wrap.
3. Add carrot and kale leaves and wrap them in the rolls.
4. Brush every roll with olive oil and put it in the hot skillet.
5. Roast the spring rolls for 20 seconds per side.
6. Sprinkle the cooked rolls with sesame seeds.

per serving: 257 calories, 6.1g protein, 47.6g carbohydrates, 4.1g fat, 2.7g fiber, 0mg cholesterol, 757mg sodium, 154mg potassium.

Faro Skillet

Yield: 4 servings | **Prep time:** 10 minutes
Cook time: 25 minutes

Ingredients:

- 1 cup cremini mushrooms, sliced
- ½ cup of water
- 1 tablespoon olive oil
- 1 teaspoon dried oregano
- ½ cup faro
- ½ cup coconut milk
- ¼ teaspoon dried thyme

Directions:

1. Roast mushrooms with olive oil in a saucepan for 10 minutes.

2. Then stir them well, and add dried oregano, dried thyme, and farro.
3. Add coconut milk and water.
4. Close the lid and simmer the meal for 15 minutes. Stir it from time to time to avoid burning.

per serving: 12 calories, 3.7g protein, 15.4g carbohydrates, 5.5g fat, 1.7g fiber, g cholesterol, 21mg sodium, 177mg potassium.

Quinoa and Scallions Balls

Yield: 4 servings | **Prep time:** 15 minutes
Cook time: 30 minutes

Ingredients:

- ½ cup quinoa, cooked
- ½ cup lean ground pork
- 3 oz scallions, chopped
- 1 egg, beaten
- 1 tablespoon almond flour
- 1 teaspoon chili flakes
- 1 cup tomato juice

Directions:

1. In the bowl mix quinoa, ground pork, scallions, egg, almond flour, and chili flakes.
2. Then make the small balls and put them in the baking pan.
3. Top the balls with tomato juice and cook in the preheated 375F oven for 30 minutes.

per serving: 177 calories,16.2g protein, 16.9g carbohydrates, 5g fat, 2g fiber, 71mg cholesterol, 204mg sodium, 462mg potassium.

BEANS

Beans

Tomato Beans

Yield: 4 servings | **Prep time:** 10 minutes
Cook time: 15 minutes

Ingredients:

- 1 ½ tablespoon olive oil
- 2 oz tomato, chopped
- ¼ teaspoon garlic, minced
- ½ white onion, diced
- ¼ cup fresh parsley, chopped
- 1 teaspoon ground cumin
- 2 cups fava beans, vanned
- 2 tablespoons apple cider vinegar

Directions:

1. Heat the olive oil in the saucepan.
2. Add onion and cook it until light brown.
3. Then add tomato, garlic, parsley, ground cumin, fava beans, and apple cider vinegar.
4. Cook the meal for 5 minutes on medium heat.

per serving: 273 calories, 20g protein, 46.1g carbohydrates, 1.9g fat, 19.5g fiber, 0mg cholesterol, 12mg sodium, 879mg potassium.

African Style Green Beans

Yield: 3 servings | **Prep time:** 15 minutes
Cook time: 7 minutes

Ingredients:

- 2 tablespoons olive oil
- 1 cup green beans
- ¼ teaspoon ground black pepper
- 1 teaspoon sesame seeds
- 1 tablespoon lemon juice
- ¼ teaspoon dried tarragon
- 1 cup of water

Directions:

1. Bring the water to a boil and put the green beans inside.
2. Boil the beans for 7 minutes. Then cool the beans in ice water and chop roughly.
3. Put the cooked green beans in the bowl, and add ground black pepper, olive oil, sesame seeds, lemon juice, and dried tarragon.
4. Stir the meal well.

per serving: 101 calories, 0.9g protein, 3g carbohydrates, 9.9g fat, 1.4g fiber, 0mg cholesterol, 5mg sodium, 90mg potassium.

Bean Wrap

Yield: 3 servings | **Prep time:** 10 minutes
Cook time: 0 minutes

Ingredients:

- 1 oz chives, chopped
- 1 tablespoon olive oil
- 1 bell pepper, sliced
- 1 cup pinto beans, canned
- 4 tablespoon dill, chopped
- 3 corn tortillas
- ½ cup Mozzarella cheese, shredded
- ½ cup lettuce

Directions:

1. Mix chives with bell pepper and olive oil.
2. Then put this mixture on the tortillas.
3. Add pinto beans, dill, Mozzarella cheese, and lettuce.
4. Roll the tortillas in the shape of the burrito.

per serving: 398 calories, 20.2g protein, 52.5g carbohydrates, 12.5g fat, 12g fiber, 20mg cholesterol, 140mg sodium, 1026mg potassium.

Lettuce and Beans Bowl

Yield: 2 servings | **Prep time:** 10 minutes
Cook time: 0 minutes

Ingredients:

- ½ cup fava beans, cooked
- 1 cup lettuce, chopped
- 1 red onion, diced
- 1 tablespoon lemon juice
- 2 tablespoons olive oil
- ½ teaspoon chili flakes

Directions:

1. Put fava beans in the bowl. Add lettuce and diced onion.
2. Shake the vegetables and sprinkle them with lemon juice, olive oil, and chili flakes.
3. Stir the meal and transfer it to the serving plates.

per serving: 274 calories, 10.7g protein, 27.5g carbohydrates, 14.7g fat, 10.7g fiber, 0mg cholesterol, 10mg sodium, 522mg potassium.

Broccoli and Beans Bowl

Yield: 4 servings | **Prep time:** 10 minutes
Cook time: 25 minutes

Ingredients:

- 1 cup broccoli, chopped
- 1 cup white cabbage, chopped
- 1 tablespoon olive oil
- ½ cup celery stalk, roughly chopped

1 teaspoon ground turmeric
1 cup haricot beans, canned
2 tablespoons tomato sauce

Directions:

1. Line the baking pan with baking paper.
2. Then mix all ingredients in the mixing bowl until homogenous.
3. Place the vegetable mixture in the baking tray, flatten, and transfer to the preheated 375F oven.
4. Bake the meal for 25 minutes. Stir the vegetables during cooking after 10 minutes of cooking.

per serving: 58 calories, 1.9g protein, 5.9g carbohydrates, 3.6g fat, 2.7g fiber, 0mg cholesterol, 67mg sodium, 276mg potassium.

Oregano Beans

Yield: 5 servings | **Prep time:** 10 minutes
Cook time: 20 minutes

Ingredients:

- 4 teaspoons avocado oil
- ½ teaspoon garlic powder
- ¼ cup chicken stock
- ½ white onion, sliced
- ¼ cup bell pepper, chopped
- 3 cups butter beans, canned
- ½ teaspoon dried oregano
- ¼ teaspoon ground cumin

Directions:

1. Heat oil in the pan and add the onion.
2. Cook it until light brown and add garlic powder, chicken stock, bell pepper, cumin, and dried oregano.
3. Simmer the ingredients for 5 minutes.
4. Add butter beans, stir the meal, and cook for 5 minutes more.

per serving: 146 calories, 6.7g protein, 20.7g carbohydrates, 4.5g fat, 5g fiber, 0mg cholesterol, 46mg sodium, 469mg potassium.

White Beans Bowl

Yield: 4 servings | **Prep time:** 10 minutes
Cook time: 25 minutes

Ingredients:

- 2 tablespoons avocado oil
- 2 garlic cloves, diced
- 2 teaspoons cajun spice mix
- 1 cup chickpeas, canned
- ½ cup tomatoes, chopped
- 1 cup white beans, chopped
- 1 cup chicken stock

Directions:

1. Pour avocado oil into the saucepan and heat it.
2. Add Cajun seasonings, garlic, and tomatoes. Cook them for 10 minutes on medium heat.
3. Then add chicken stock, white beans, and chickpeas.
4. Close the lid and cook the meal for 10 minutes on low heat.
5. Transfer the meal to the serving bowls.

per serving: 259 calories, 10.6g protein, 33.9g carbohydrates, 10.3g fat, 9.9g fiber, 0mg cholesterol, 206mg sodium, 558mg potassium.

Tender Garlic Dip

Yield: 6 servings | **Prep time:** 10 minutes
Cook time: 5 minutes

Ingredients:

- 2 cups cannellini beans, cooked
- 1 tablespoon olive oil, softened
- 1 teaspoon garlic, minced
- 2 tablespoons lime juice

Directions:

1. Roast cooked cannellini beans and olive oil for 5 minutes.
2. Then sprinkle the beans with lime juice and garlic.
3. Blend the beans with the help of the immersion blender until smooth.

per serving: 227 calories, 14.6g protein, 37.3g carbohydrates, 2.9g fat, 15.3g fiber, 0mg cholesterol, 16mg sodium, 874mg potassium.

Beans and Meat Stew

Yield: 12 servings | **Prep time:** 5 minutes
Cook time: 55 minutes

Ingredients:

- 2 pounds beef sirloin, chopped
- 2 cups white beans, soaked
- 1 cup tomatoes, chopped
- 1 teaspoon cayenne pepper
- 1 teaspoon salt
- 1 cup fresh parsley, chopped
- 4 cups of water

Directions:

1. Put all ingredients in the stew pot and transfer them to the oven.
2. Cook the stew at 365F for 55 minutes.
3. Then stir the stew well.

per serving: 328 calories, 24.7g protein, 19.5g carbohydrates, 16.6g fat, 4.9g fiber, 68mg cholesterol, 253mg sodium, 712mg potassium.

Beans and Tomatoes Ragout

Yield: 5 servings | **Prep time:** 10 minutes
Cook time: 10 minutes

Ingredients:

- 1 cup okra, chopped, cooked
- ½ teaspoon ground paprika
- 1 cup red kidney beans, cooked
- 2 tomatoes, chopped
- 2 tablespoons olive oil
- 1 tablespoon lemon juice
- ½ avocado, chopped

Directions:

1. Put okra and red kidney beans in the big bowl.
2. Sprinkle the ingredients with olive oil and ground paprika.
3. Add tomatoes, lemon juice, and avocado.
4. Stir the meal and bake in the baking pan for 10 minutes at 375F.

per serving: 241 calories, 9.6g protein, 29.5g carbohydrates, 10.2g fat, 8.5g fiber, 0mg cholesterol, 7mg sodium, 854mg potassium.

Meat and Garbanzo Beans

Yield: 5 servings | **Prep time:** 10 minutes
Cook time: 10 minutes

Ingredients:

- 10 oz beef loin, chopped
- 1 teaspoon Cajun seasonings
- 2 tablespoons avocado oil
- 1 cup garbanzo beans, cooked

Directions:

1. Rub the beef loin with Cajun seasonings and brush with 1 tablespoon of avocado oil.
2. Grill the meat for 5 minutes per side at 400F.
3. Then cut the meat into thin strips and mix it with garbanzo beans and the remaining avocado oil.

per serving: 299 calories, 24.9g protein, 24.3g carbohydrates, 11.6g fat, 7g fiber, 51mg cholesterol, 57mg sodium, 578mg potassium.

Garlic Beans

Yield: 3 servings | **Prep time:** 10 minutes
Cook time: 45 minutes

Ingredients:

- 1 tablespoon avocado oil
- 1 onion, chopped
- 1 teaspoon garlic, minced
- 7 oz beef sirloin, chopped
- 1 cup green beans, chopped, boiled

- 2 tomatoes, chopped
- ½ cup of water

Directions:

1. Roast the meat with avocado oil in the saucepan for 2 minutes per side.
2. Then add onion and garlic. Stir the ingredients and cook for 1 minute more.
3. Then add white beans, tomatoes, and water.
4. Stir gently, close the lid, and simmer the meal on low heat for 40 minutes.

per serving: 201 calories, 21.8g protein, 8.7g carbohydrates, 8.8g fat, 2.6g fiber, 59mg cholesterol, 59mg sodium, 515mg potassium.

Tomato Green Beans

Yield: 4 servings | **Prep time:** 10 minutes
Cook time: 10 minutes

Ingredients:

- 2 cups green beans
- 1 cup of water
- 1 teaspoon chili flakes
- ½ teaspoon onion powder
- 1 tablespoon apple cider vinegar
- 1 tablespoon fresh cilantro, chopped
- 2 tablespoons tomato paste

Directions:

1. Boil the green beans in water for 10 minutes.
2. Then cool the beans and put them in the mixing bowl.
3. Add chili flakes, onion powder, apple cider vinegar, fresh cilantro, and tomato paste.
4. Carefully mix the green beans.

per serving: 43 calories, 3g protein, 6.9g carbohydrates, 0.5g fat, 2g fiber, 2mg cholesterol, 29mg sodium, 222mg potassium.

Festive Stuffing

Yield: 4 servings | **Prep time:** 5 minutes
Cook time: 15 minutes

Ingredients:

- 1 cup cannellini beans, cooked
- ½ cup zucchini, chopped
- 2 tomatoes
- 1 teaspoon chili powder
- 1 jalapeno pepper, chopped
- ½ cup chicken stock

Directions:

1. Bring the chicken stock to a boil and add tomatoes, chili powder, jalapeno pepper, and zucchini.

2. Simmer the ingredients for 5 minutes.
3. Then add cannellini beans and cook the stuffing with an open lid for 10 minutes.

per serving: 168 calories, 11.1g protein, 30.8g carbohydrates, 0.8g fat, 7.8g fiber, 0mg cholesterol, 117mg sodium, 765mg potassium.

Thyme Beans

Yield: 4 servings | Prep time: 10 minutes
Cook time: 5 minutes

Ingredients:

- 6 oz black beans, boiled
- 1 tablespoon olive oil
- 1 tablespoon apple cider vinegar
- 1 teaspoon dried thyme
- 3 tablespoons tomato paste
- ½ teaspoon dried rosemary
- 1 tablespoon avocado oil

Directions:

1. Preheat the grill to 400F.
2. Sprinkle the black beans with olive oil and add tomato paste. Mix the ingredients.
3. Place the mixture in the pan and add olive oil. Cook the mixture for 2 minutes per side.
4. Then transfer the beans to the serving bowls.
5. Sprinkle them with thyme, apple cider vinegar, and rosemary.
6. Shake the meal gently.

per serving: 92 calories, 1.6g protein, 7g carbohydrates, 7.2g fat, 2.7g fiber, 0mg cholesterol, 8mg sodium, 316mg potassium.

Beans and Seafood Salad

Yield: 4 servings | Prep time: 5 minutes
Cook time: 5 minutes

Ingredients:

- 1 cup white beans, cooked
- 4 oz shrimp, peeled
- ¼ teaspoon ground cumin
- ½ teaspoon lemon juice
- 1 tablespoon olive oil
- 1 teaspoon sesame seeds
- 1 tablespoon avocado oil

Directions:

1. Heat the olive oil in the skillet.
2. Then sprinkle the shrimp with ground cumin and put in the hot oil.
3. Roast them for 2 minutes per side.
4. Transfer the cooked shrimp to the salad bowl.
5. Add white beans, lemon juice, sesame seeds, and

avocado oil.
6. Gently stir the cooked meal.

per serving: 219 calories, 15.3g protein, 29.3g carbohydrates, 4.9g fat, 7.2g fiber, 9mg cholesterol, 52mg sodium, 732mg potassium.

Simple Meat and Beans Soup

Yield: 4 servings | Prep time: 10 minutes
Cook time: 25 minutes

Ingredients:

- 4 cups water
- 5 oz beef loin, chopped
- 1 cup red kidney beans, cooked
- 1 carrot, chopped
- 1 tablespoon olive oil
- 1 celery stalk, chopped

Directions:

1. Roast the celery stalk with olive oil in the skillet until light brown.
2. Bring the water to a boil, and add beef loin, celery stalk, carrot, and red kidney beans.
3. Simmer the soup for 20 minutes.

per serving: 212 calories, 11.5g protein, 33g carbohydrates, 4.6g fat, 8g fiber, 0mg cholesterol, 781mg sodium, 729mg potassium.

Bean Pate

Yield: 8 servings | Prep time: 15 minutes
Cook time: 0 minutes

Ingredients:

- 3 cups white beans, cooked
- 1 tablespoon coconut oil, melted
- 1 tablespoon scallions, chopped
- ½ teaspoon ground turmeric
- ¼ teaspoon salt

Directions:

1. Put all ingredients in the blender and blend until smooth.
2. Transfer the paste to the bowl, flatten the surface of it, and leave it in the fridge for 10 minutes.

per serving: 268 calories, 17.7g protein, 45.8g carbohydrates, 2.4g fat, 11.6g fiber, 0mg cholesterol, 13mg sodium, 1365mg potassium.

Lunch Bean Spread

Yield: 6 servings | Prep time: 15 minutes
Cook time: 0 minutes

Ingredients:

- 10 oz white beans, cooked

- 2 oz Feta cheese, crumbled
- 1 tablespoon olive oil
- 1 teaspoon dried mint
- 1 teaspoon apple cider vinegar

Directions:

1. Mash the white beans with the help of the potato masher.
2. Then add olive oil, dried mint, and apple cider vinegar.
3. Stir the mashed beans mixture well and add Feta cheese.
4. Carefully mix the spread.

per serving: 225 calories, 12.1g protein, 30.1g carbohydrates, 6.4g fat, 6.9g fiber, 10mg cholesterol, 39mg sodium, 9mg potassium.

Cannellini Beans and Cucumber Mix

Yield: 4 servings | **Prep time:** 10 minutes
Cook time: 0 minutes

Ingredients:

- 1 cup cucumber, chopped
- 1 cup arugula, chopped
- ½ cup corn kernels, cooked
- ½ cup fresh dill, chopped
- 1 cup cannellini beans, cooked

Directions:

1. Put all ingredients in the mixing bowl and carefully mix.
2. Then transfer the mix to the serving bowls.
3. Add olive oil, if desired.

per serving: 222 calories, 12.9g protein, 43.7g carbohydrates, 1.4g fat, 11.2g fiber, 0mg cholesterol, 16mg sodium, 1064mg potassium.

Bean Mix

Yield: 8 servings | **Prep time:** 10 minutes
Cook time: 0 minutes

Ingredients:

- 1 cup canned cannellini beans, drained
- 1 cup canned red kidney beans, drained
- 1 cup canned white beans, drained
- 1 red onion, diced
- 3 tablespoons avocado oil
- ½ teaspoon dried cilantro
- 1 teaspoon lemon juice
- ½ teaspoon apple cider vinegar
- 1 carrot, grated

Directions:

1. Make the dressing: mix apple cider vinegar, lemon

juice, dried cilantro, and avocado oil in a shallow bowl.
2. Then mix all remaining ingredients in the mixing bowl.
3. Add dressing, shake well, and transfer the meal to the serving plates.

per serving: 292 calories, 16.7g protein, 45.2g carbohydrates, 5.9g fat, 13.6g fiber, 0mg cholesterol, 18mg sodium, 1134mg potassium.

Greek-Style Baked Beans

Yield: 4 servings | **Prep time:** 10 minutes
Cook time: 0 minutes

Ingredients:

- ½ cup white beans, boiled
- ½ cup chickpeas, boiled
- 3 oz Parmesan, grated
- ½ teaspoon olive oil
- ½ teaspoon ground cumin

Directions:

1. Place the beans and chickpeas in the tray.
2. Sprinkle the ingredients with olive oil and ground cumin. Bake them for 5 minutes at 375F.
3. Then top the ingredients with Parmesan and bake for 5 minutes more.
4. Serve the meal with yogurt.

per serving: 173 calories, 6g protein, 22g carbohydrates, 7.5g fat, 5.2g fiber, 0mg cholesterol, 3mg sodium, 520mg potassium.

Bean and Mozzarella Dip

Yield: 6 servings | **Prep time:** 10 minutes
Cook time: 0 minutes

Ingredients:

- 6 oz white beans, boiled
- 1 avocado, peeled and chopped
- 1 oz Mozzarella, grated
- 1 teaspoon smoked paprika

Directions:

1. Blend the white bean and avocado in the blender until smooth.
2. Then transfer the mixture to the bowl, and add Mozzarella and smoked paprika.
3. Carefully stir the dip with the help of the spoon.

per serving: 178 calories, 8.8g protein, 20.2g carbohydrates, 7.8g fat, 6.6g fiber, 3mg cholesterol, 50mg sodium, 672mg potassium.

Grilled Cod with Edamame Beans

Yield: 4 servings | **Prep time:** 10 minutes
Cook time: 14 minutes

Ingredients:

- 1-pound cod fillet
- ½ teaspoon dried parsley
- ½ teaspoon ground coriander
- 1 tablespoon avocado oil
- ¼ cup edamame beans, boiled
- 1 tablespoon mustard

Directions:

1. Place the edamame beans on cod filler.
2. Then fold the fillet and secure the cut with toothpicks.
3. After this, gently rub the fish with parsley, ground coriander, avocado oil, and mustard.
4. Preheat the grill to 390F.
5. Put the fish on the preheated grill and cook it for 7 minutes per side.

per serving: 215 calories, 24.2g protein, 3.1g carbohydrates, 12.1g fat, 1.2g fiber, 50mg cholesterol, 105mg sodium, 456mg potassium.

Coriander Black Beans

Yield: 4 servings | **Prep time:** 10 minutes
Cook time: 11 minutes

Ingredients:

- 1 cup black beans, boiled
- 1 teaspoon coriander seeds
- 1 teaspoon dried rosemary
- 2 tablespoons avocado oil

Directions:

1. Heat the pan and put coriander seeds inside.
2. Roast them for 3 minutes on medium heat.
3. Then add avocado oil, dried rosemary, and black beans.
4. Roast the ingredients for 8 minutes. Stir the meal every 2 minutes.

per serving: 178 calories, 10.7g protein, 31.1g carbohydrates, 1.7g fat, 7.8g fiber, 0mg cholesterol, 4mg sodium, 754mg potassium.

Winter Beans Stew

Yield: 6 servings | **Prep time:** 10 minutes
Cook time: 70 minutes

Ingredients:

- 1 teaspoon ground paprika
- 1 teaspoon ground turmeric
- 2 cups white beans
- 8 cups of water
- 1 tablespoon canola oil
- 1 bell pepper, diced
- 2 oz tomato paste

Directions:

1. Heat canola oil in the saucepan.
2. Add bell pepper and roast it for 3 minutes.
3. After this, add white beans, ground paprika, ground turmeric, and tomato paste.
4. Add water and close the lid.
5. Simmer the stew for 65 minutes on medium-low heat.

per serving: 260 calories, 16.4g protein, 44.2g carbohydrates, 3.1g fat, 11.1g fiber, 0mg cholesterol, 30mg sodium, 1356mg potassium.

Stir-Fried Snap Peas

Yield: 4 servings | **Prep time:** 10 minutes
Cook time: 20 minutes

Ingredients:

- 1-pound snap peas
- 1 tablespoon olive oil
- 1 teaspoon dried dill
- ¼ cup of water
- 1 teaspoon apple cider vinegar

Directions:

1. Put the snap peas in the hot saucepan.
2. Add water and cook the vegetables for 10 minutes on low heat.
3. Add canola oil, and dried dill, and stir well.
4. Cook the snap peas for 10 minutes more.
5. When the vegetables are soft, they are cooked.
6. Sprinkle the snap peas with apple cider vinegar and transfer them to the plates.

per serving: 66 calories, 2.1g protein, 8.5g carbohydrates, 3.6g fat, 4g fiber, 0mg cholesterol, 8mg sodium, 243mg potassium.

Beans and Pepper

Yield: 2 servings | **Prep time:** 10 minutes
Cook time: 7 minutes

Ingredients:

- 4 oz white beans, cooked
- ¼ cup quinoa
- 1 cup water
- 1 sweet pepper, diced
- 1 tablespoon olive oil
- ¼ teaspoon garlic powder

Directions:

1. Bring the water to a boil and add quinoa.

2. Cook it for 5 minutes.
3. Then add garlic powder, sweet pepper, and white beans.
4. Add olive oil, carefully stir the ingredients, and cook the meal for 1 minute.

per serving: 249 calories, 10.4g protein, 26.9g carbohydrates, 11.8g fat, 5.4g fiber, 0mg cholesterol, 607mg sodium, 243mg potassium.

Pear and Beans

Yield: 6 servings | **Prep time:** 10 minutes
Cook time: 35 minutes

Ingredients:

- 2 cups red kidney beans, boiled
- ½ cup fresh parsley, chopped
- 2 pears, chopped
- 1 teaspoon ground cinnamon
- 1 carrot, chopped
- 3 tablespoons avocado oil
- 1 cup of water

Directions:

1. Heat avocado oil in the saucepan.
2. Add parsley, pear, cinnamon, and carrot.
3. Roast the ingredients for 10 minutes on low heat.
4. Then add water and red kidney beans.
5. Cook the meal for 25 minutes on medium heat.

per serving: 151 calories, 8.4g protein, 27.9g carbohydrates, 1.7g fat, 8.6g fiber, 0mg cholesterol, 413mg sodium, 553mg potassium.

Green Beans Soup

Yield: 5 servings | **Prep time:** 10 minutes
Cook time: 20 minutes

Ingredients:

- 1 teaspoon dried oregano
- 1 cup Greek yogurt
- 10 oz green beans, trimmed, chopped, frozen
- 2 cups water

Directions:

1. Put all ingredients in the big saucepan and close the lid.
2. Simmer the soup for 20 minutes on low heat.

per serving: 307 calories, 23.1g protein, 52g carbohydrates, 1.6g fat, 12.9g fiber, 2mg cholesterol, 43mg sodium, 1575mg potassium.

VEGETABLES

Vegetables

Spinach Mix

Yield: 5 servings | **Prep time:** 10 minutes
Cook time: 20 minutes

Ingredients:

- 1-pound spinach, roughly chopped
- ½ cup tomatoes, chopped
- ½ teaspoon minced garlic
- ½ teaspoon ground white pepper
- 3 tablespoons olive oil
- 1 oz Mozzarella, grated
- ½ teaspoon dried oregano

Directions:

1. Heat the olive oil, and add spinach and tomatoes.
2. Sprinkle the ingredients with dried oregano, ground white pepper, and minced garlic.
3. Fry the vegetables for 15 minutes on medium-low heat.
4. Then sprinkle the cooked vegetables with grated Mozzarella.

per serving: 109 calories, 3.2g protein, 4.3g carbohydrates, 9.6g fat, 3.2g fiber, 4mg cholesterol, 74mg sodium, 334mg potassium.

Garlic Zucchini

Yield: 4 servings | **Prep time:** 10 minutes
Cook time: 15 minutes

Ingredients:

- 1 zucchini, chopped
- 5 tablespoons olive oil
- ½ cup white onion, diced
- 1 teaspoon garlic powder
- ½ teaspoon dried cilantro
- 3 oz Plain yogurt

Directions:

1. Sprinkle the chopped zucchini with garlic powder.
2. Preheat the olive oil in the saucepan and add the onion.
3. Cook it for 3 minutes.
4. Then add chopped zucchini and roast the vegetables for 10 minutes on medium heat. Stir them from time to time.
5. Then transfer the cooked vegetables to the big bowl.
6. Add dried cilantro and Plain yogurt.
7. Carefully mix the meal.

per serving: 207 calories, 2.6g protein, 10.2g carbohydrates, 18g fat, 4.4g fiber, 1mg cholesterol, 18mg sodium, 345mg potassium.

Tender Basil Artichoke

Yield: 4 servings | **Prep time:** 10 minutes
Cook time: 10 minutes

Ingredients:

- ½ teaspoon ginger, peeled, grated
- ½ teaspoon salt
- ½ teaspoon ground black pepper
- ¼ cup coconut milk
- 1 cup artichoke hearts, frozen
- 1 tablespoon olive oil
- 2 teaspoons fresh basil, chopped

Directions:

1. Heat a pan with oil over medium-high heat, and add ginger and water.
2. Cook the liquid for 1 minute.
3. Add all remaining ingredients and stir well.
4. Cook the meal for 9 minutes with a closed lid.

per serving: 40 calories, 0.5g protein, 1.5g carbohydrates, 3.4g fat, 1g fiber, 0mg cholesterol, 304mg sodium, 14mg potassium.

Chili Cauliflower

Yield: 4 servings | **Prep time:** 10 minutes
Cook time: 10 minutes

Ingredients:

- 1 cup cauliflower, roughly chopped
- 1 teaspoon chili powder
- 1 tablespoon coconut oil
- 1 bell pepper, diced

Directions:

1. Heat the coconut oil in the skillet.
2. Add cauliflower and roast it for 5 minutes.
3. Then sprinkle the vegetables with chili powder and bell pepper.
4. Stir the ingredients carefully and close the lid.
5. Cook the meal for 5 minutes more.

per serving: 58 calories, 1.4g protein, 5.2g carbohydrates, 4.3g fat, 1.7g fiber, 0mg cholesterol, 17mg sodium, 191mg potassium.

Broccoli Rice

Yield: 4 servings | **Prep time:** 5 minutes
Cook time: 10 minutes

Ingredients:

- 2 cups broccoli, shredded
- 1 tablespoon coconut oil
- 1 oz Parmesan, grated
- 1 cup chicken stock

Directions:

1. Bring the chicken stock to a boil and add shredded broccoli.
2. Boil it for 5 minutes.
3. Then drain the liquid and mix broccoli with coconut oil and Parmesan.
4. Stir the meal carefully.

per serving: 63 calories, 3.5g protein, 3.1g carbohydrates, 4.6g fat, 1.3g fiber, 13mg cholesterol, 292mg sodium, 156mg potassium.

Grilled Ruby Chard

Yield: 2 servings | Prep time: 5 minutes
Cook time: 5 minutes

Ingredients:

- 2 cups ruby chard, roughly chopped
- 1 tablespoon sesame seeds oil
- 1 oz Parmesan, grated
- ½ cup cream cheese

Directions:

1. Place the ruby chard in the preheated to 400F grill, sprinkle with sesame oil, and grill for 5 minutes.
2. Transfer the ruby chard to the bowl and add cream cheese, stirring the meal.
3. Saute the meal for 5 minutes.
4. Then sprinkle the cooked meal with Parmesan.

per serving: 128 calories, 0.7g protein, 2.3g carbohydrates, 11.4g fat, 0g fiber, 11mg cholesterol, 20mg sodium, 30mg potassium.

Ginger Broccoli Florets

Yield: 3 servings | Prep time: 10 minutes
Cook time: 9 minutes

Ingredients:

1-pound broccoli, cut into florets
1 cup of water
1 tablespoon olive oil
1 teaspoon ground ginger

Directions:

1. Bring the water to a boil and put the broccoli inside.
2. Boil it for 6 minutes.
3. Meanwhile, heat the olive oil well.
4. Add the boiled broccoli and sprinkle with ground ginger.
5. Roast the broccoli florets for 1 minute per side.

per serving: 78 calories, 3g protein, 8.1g carbohydrates, 4.7g fat, 3.8g fiber, 0mg cholesterol, 48mg sodium, 162mg potassium.

Coriander Carrots

Yield: 4 servings | Prep time: 10 minutes
Cook time: 17 minutes

Ingredients:

- 3 tablespoons olive oil
- 4 carrots, sliced
- 1/3 cup plain yogurt
- 1 teaspoon ground coriander

Directions:

1. Roast the sliced carrot with olive oil for 3 minutes per side.
2. Then sprinkle the carrot with plain yogurt, and ground coriander.
3. Carefully stir the vegetables and close the lid.
4. Cook the meal for 10 minutes on medium heat.

per serving: 56 calories, 1.9g protein, 8.3g carbohydrates, 1.7g fat, 2.1g fiber, 1mg cholesterol, 58mg sodium, 286mg potassium.

Thyme Baked Potatoes

Yield: 4 servings | Prep time: 10 minutes
Cook time: 20 minutes

Ingredients:

- 4 Russet potatoes, halved
- 1 teaspoon dried thyme
- 2 tablespoons canola oil

Directions:

1. Pierce the potato halves with the help of the fork and sprinkle with canola oil and dried thyme.
2. Wrap every potato half in the foil and bake in the preheated 385F oven for 20 minutes.

per serving: 210 calories, 4.1g protein, 34.1g carbohydrates, 7.1g fat, 3.8g fiber, 0mg cholesterol, 13mg sodium, 975mg potassium.

Cinnamon Butternut Squash

Yield: 6 servings | Prep time: 10 minutes
Cook time: 30 minutes

Ingredients:

- 3 tablespoons olive oil
- ½ teaspoon vanilla extract
- 12 oz baby butternut squash, sliced
- 1 teaspoon ground cinnamon

Directions:

1. Brush the casserole mold with olive oil and put the baby squash inside in one layer.
2. Then top the vegetables with vanilla extract and ground cinnamon. Mix the squash gently.

3. Wrap the casserole mold in the foil and bake in the preheated 375F oven for 30 minutes.

per serving: 214 calories, 9.2g protein, 22g carbohydrates, 10.8g fat, 6.4g fiber, 5mg cholesterol, 39mg sodium, 557mg potassium.

Parsley Mushrooms

Yield: 4 servings | **Prep time:** 10 minutes
Cook time: 20 minutes

Ingredients:

- 3 oz fresh parsley, chopped
- 1 tablespoon olive oil
- 8 oz Shiitake mushrooms, chopped
- ½ teaspoon ground black pepper
- ¼ cup Cheddar cheese
- 1 cup chicken stock

Directions:

1. Put olive oil in the pan and preheat.
2. Then add Shiitake mushrooms.
3. Sprinkle them with ground black pepper and cook for 15 minutes on medium heat.
4. Add chicken stock and close the lid.
5. Cook the mushrooms for 5 minutes and add cheddar cheese.
6. Carefully stir the meal and cook it for 2 minutes.

per serving: 119 calories, 3.5 protein, 7.1g carbohydrates, 8.9g fat, 1.5g fiber, 15mg cholesterol, 260mg sodium, 256mg potassium.

Lime Snap Peas

Yield: 6 servings | **Prep time:** 5 minutes
Cook time: 15 minutes

Ingredients:

- 3 teaspoons lime juice
- 1 teaspoon lime zest, grated
- 1 tablespoon avocado oil
- ½ cup of water
- ¼ teaspoon garlic powder
- 2 cups sugar snap peas
- ¼ teaspoon ground turmeric

Directions:

1. Roast the snap peas with avocado oil for 2 minutes.
2. Stir them and add lime zest, garlic powder, lime juice, and ground turmeric.
3. Cook the snap peas for 3 minutes more.
4. Then add water and close the lid.
5. Boil the snap peas for 10 minutes on medium heat.

per serving: 30 calories, 0.7g protein, 1.9g carbohydrates, 2.3g fat, 0.6g fiber, 0mg cholesterol, 2mg sodium, 50mg potassium.

Chili Corn

Yield: 4 servings | **Prep time:** 5 minutes
Cook time: 8 minutes

Ingredients:

- 4 corn on the cobs
- 4 teaspoons avocado oil
- ½ teaspoon chili powder

Directions:

1. Preheat the grill to 400F.
2. Rub the corn on the cobs with avocado oil and gril them for 4 minutes per side.
3. Then sprinkle the vegetables with chili powder.

per serving: 93 calories, 2g protein, 14.2g carbohydrates 4.3g fat, 1.8g fiber, 10mg cholesterol, 30mg sodium 160mg potassium.

Seasoned Chickpeas

Yield: 2 servings | **Prep time:** 10 minutes
Cook time: 25 minutes

Ingredients:

- ½ garlic clove, diced
- ½ cup chickpeas, boiled
- 1 tablespoon avocado oil
- ¼ cup of water
- 1 teaspoon Italian seasonings

Directions:

1. Mix garlic with chickpeas and avocado oil and cook over medium heat for 5 minutes.
2. Then transfer the ingredients to the baking pan.
3. Add water and Italian seasonings.
4. Transfer the pan with chickpeas to the oven and bake at 365F for 20 minutes.

per serving: 260 calories, 10g protein, 33.2g carbohydrates, 10.8g fat, 9.3g fiber, 2mg cholesterol 15mg sodium, 479mg potassium.

Thyme Carrot

Yield: 4 servings | **Prep time:** 5 minutes
Cook time: 30 minutes

Ingredients:

- 2 cups carrot, chopped
- 1 teaspoon dried thyme
- ½ cup coconut milk
- ½ teaspoon salt

Directions:

1. Put all ingredients in the saucepan and close the lid
2. Simmer the carrot on low-medium heat for 30 minutes.

per serving: 31 calories, 0.6g protein, 6.6g carbohydrates, 0.4g fat, 1.5g fiber, 0mg cholesterol, 346mg sodium, 179mg potassium.

Basil Fennel

Yield: 4 servings | **Prep time:** 10 minutes
Cook time: 15 minutes

Ingredients:

- 1 lime slice, chopped
- 1 teaspoon dried basil
- 2 tablespoons olive oil
- 1-pound fennel bulb, peeled, roughly chopped

Directions:

1. Line the baking tray with baking paper.
2. Then put fennel in it and sprinkle it with lime, dried basil, and olive oil.
3. Mix the fennel and bake in the oven at 375F for 15 minutes or until the fennel is tender.

per serving: 98 calories, 1.4g protein, 8.4g carbohydrates, 7.2g fat, 3.6g fiber, 0mg cholesterol, 59mg sodium, 472mg potassium.

Tender Leek Spread

Yield: 4 servings | **Prep time:** 10 minutes
Cook time: 20 minutes

Ingredients:

- 2 cups leek, chopped
- ¼ cup coconut milk
- 2 tablespoons cream cheese
- ¼ cup water
- 1 tablespoon olive oil

Directions:

1. Roast the leek with olive oil for 2-3 minutes in the saucepan.
2. Add cream cheese and coconut milk.
3. Stir the ingredients and saute them for 15 minutes on low heat.
4. Gently mash the leek and transfer it to the serving bowls.

per serving: 71 calories, 0.9g protein, 6.6g carbohydrates, 4.9g fat, 0.8g fiber, 3mg cholesterol, 60mg sodium, 92mg potassium.

Provolone Cheese Asparagus

Yield: 4 servings | **Prep time:** 10 minutes
Cook time: 5 minutes

Ingredients:

- 1-pound asparagus, trimmed
- 2 oz provolone cheese, grated

- 2 tablespoons olive oil
- 1 teaspoon smoked paprika

Directions:

1. Sprinkle the asparagus with olive oil and smoked paprika.
2. Then arrange the vegetables on the grill and cook for 2 minutes per side.
3. Then transfer the cooked asparagus to the plates and top with grated Provolone cheese.

per serving: 130 calories, 7.1g protein, 5.3g carbohydrates, 10.2g fat, 2.5g fiber, 10mg cholesterol, 134mg sodium, 236mg potassium.

Fragrant Pickles

Yield: 4 servings | **Prep time:** 10 minutes
Cook time: 0 minutes

Ingredients:

- ½ cup pickled cucumbers, chopped
- 1 garlic clove, diced
- 1 chili pepper, chopped
- ½ cup fresh dill, chopped
- 1 tablespoon apple cider vinegar
- 1 tablespoon olive oil

Directions:

1. Mix chopped pickled cucumber with diced garlic and chili pepper.
2. Then add dill.
3. Sprinkle the vegetables with apple cider vinegar and olive oil.
4. Gently shake the mixture before serving.

per serving: 45 calories, 0.5g protein, 3.4g carbohydrates, 3.6g fat, 0.8g fiber, 0mg cholesterol, 3mg sodium, 80mg potassium.

Almonds and Greens Bowl

Yield: 3 servings | **Prep time:** 10 minutes
Cook time: 0 minutes

Ingredients:

- 1 cup lettuce, chopped
- 1 cup fresh arugula, chopped
- ½ cup cherry tomatoes, halved
- 2 oz almonds, chopped
- 1 tablespoon olive oil
- 2 oz gorgonzola cheese, crumbled

Directions:

1. In the big bowl mix lettuce, arugula, and cherry tomatoes.
2. Sprinkle the greens with olive oil and shake.
3. Then transfer the mixture to the serving plates and

top with almonds and gorgonzola.

per serving: 222 calories, 9.7g protein, 6g carbohydrates, 19.4g fat, 2.9g fiber, 18mg cholesterol, 251mg sodium, 285mg potassium.

Garlic and Hazelnuts Beets

Yield: 4 servings | **Prep time:** 10 minutes
Cook time: 60 minutes

Ingredients:

- 1-pound beets, peeled
- 1 teaspoon minced garlic
- 2 tablespoons olive oil
- 2 oz hazelnuts, chopped
- 1 teaspoon fresh parsley, chopped
- 3 cups of water

Directions:

1. Boil the beets in water for 50 minutes or until the vegetables are soft.
2. Then drain the water and slice the beets.
3. Put the sliced beets in the saucepan, and add ¼ cup of hot water (from the beets).
4. Then add minced garlic, oil, hazelnuts, and parsley.
5. Close the lid and braise the meal for 10 minutes more.

per serving: 114 calories, 2.1g protein, 11.8g carbohydrates, 7.2g fat, 2.4g fiber, 0mg cholesterol, 88mg sodium, 359mg potassium.

Thyme Sweet Potato

Yield: 4 servings | **Prep time:** 15 minutes
Cook time: 35 minutes

Ingredients:

- 2 cups sweet potatoes, peeled, roughly chopped
- 1 onion, peeled, diced
- 1 teaspoon dried thyme
- 2 tablespoons olive oil
- 2 tablespoons plain yogurt

Directions:

1. Put the sweet potatoes, and onion in the baking tray.
2. Sprinkle the vegetables with dried thyme and olive oil. Shake the ingredients well.
3. Bake the sweet potato mixture for 35 minutes at 365F.
4. Transfer the cooked meal to the serving plates and top with plain yogurt.

per serving: 247 calories, 6.5g protein, 37g carbohydrates, 8.8g fat, 7.6g fiber, 0mg cholesterol, 18mg sodium, 854mg potassium.

Honey Butternut Squash Slices

Yield: 2 servings | **Prep time:** 10 minutes
Cook time: 10 minutes

Ingredients:

- 6 oz butternut squash, sliced
- 1 teaspoon liquid honey
- 1 tablespoon lemon juice

Directions:

1. Grill the vegetables in the preheated to 400F grill for 4 minutes per side.
2. Sprinkle the grilled butternut squash slices with liquid honey and lemon juice.

per serving: 60 calories, 0.9g protein, 10g carbohydrates, 2.4g fat, 1.7g fiber, 0mg cholesterol, 4mg sodium, 306mg potassium.

Turmeric Zucchini Rounds

Yield: 4 servings | **Prep time:** 20 minutes
Cook time: 4 minutes

Ingredients:

- 2 large zucchinis, roughly sliced
- 1 teaspoon salt
- 1 teaspoon ground turmeric
- 3 tablespoons avocado oil

Directions:

1. Rub the zucchini slices (rounds) with salt and leave for 10 minutes.
2. Then mix ground turmeric with avocado oil and brush every zucchini slice with this mixture.
3. Place the zucchini rounds in the preheated to 390F grill and cook them for 2 minutes per side.

per serving: 160 calories, 2.7g protein, 16.4g carbohydrates, 11g fat, 9.7g fiber, 0mg cholesterol, 587mg sodium, 634mg potassium.

Purple Cabbage Salad

Yield: 5 servings | **Prep time:** 10 minutes
Cook time: 0 minutes

Ingredients:

- 3 cups purple cabbage, shredded
- 1 carrot, peeled, grated
- 1 cup Plain yogurt
- 1 teaspoon ground black pepper

Directions:

1. Put all ingredients in the mixing bowl and mix well.

per serving: 32 calories, 1.3g protein, 5g carbohydrates, 1.2g fat, 1.5g fiber, 2mg cholesterol, 472mg sodium, 131mg potassium

Thyme Tomato Shish

Yield: 4 servings | Prep time: 10 minutes
Cook time: 5 minutes

Ingredients:

- 6 tomatoes
- 1 tablespoon olive oil
- ½ teaspoon dried thyme
- ¼ teaspoon ground black pepper

Directions:

1. Chop the tomatoes roughly and sting them in the skewers.
2. Sprinkle the vegetables with ground black pepper, dried thyme, and olive oil.
3. Grill the shish for 2 minutes per side in the preheated 400F grill.

per serving: 80 calories, 2g protein, 11.2g carbohydrates, 3.9g fat, 3.1g fiber, 0mg cholesterol, 157mg sodium, 146mg potassium

Radish and Arugula Bowl

Yield: 4 servings | Prep time: 10 minutes
Cook time: 0 minutes

Ingredients:

- 1 cup radish, chopped
- 2 cups arugula, chopped
- 1 teaspoon pumpkin seeds
- ½ teaspoon sesame seeds
- ¼ cup Plain yogurt
- 2 tablespoons lemon juice

Directions:

1. Mix radish and arugula.
2. Add pumpkin seeds, sesame seeds, Plain yogurt, and lemon juice.
3. Carefully mix all ingredients and transfer them to the serving bowls.

per serving: 90 calories, 3.9g protein, 17.2g carbohydrates, 1.6g fat, 2.9g fiber, 1mg cholesterol, 35mg sodium, 335mg potassium

Feta and Dill Beets

Yield: 4 servings | Prep time: 10 minutes
Cook time: 0 minutes

Ingredients:

- 1-pound beets, baked, peeled, cubed
- 2 tablespoons olive oil
- 1 tablespoon dried dill
- 1 cup Feta cheese, crumbled

Directions:

1. Mix dried dill and olive oil.
2. Then mix beets with Feta cheese.
3. Sprinkle the beets with the olive oil mixture and shake gently.

per serving: 234 calories, 9.3g protein, 12.3g carbohydrates, 17.1g fat, 2.4g fiber, 25mg cholesterol, 558mg sodium, 439mg potassium

Pesto Cauliflower

Yield: 5 servings | Prep time: 10 minutes
Cook time: 10 minutes

Ingredients:

- 3 cups cauliflower, chopped
- ¼ cup pesto sauce
- 2 oz Cheddar cheese, shredded
- 3 cups of water

Directions:

1. Bring the water to a boil.
2. Add cauliflower and boil for 10 minutes.
3. Then drain the water and cool the cauliflower.
4. Mix it with pesto sauce and shake it well.
5. Transfer the cauliflower to the plate and sprinkle it with Cheddar cheese.

per serving: 89 calories, 5.5g protein, 4.4g carbohydrates, 5.8g fat, 1.4g fiber, 8mg cholesterol, 162mg sodium, 174mg potassium

Dill Mashed Potato

Yield: 4 servings | Prep time: 10 minutes
Cook time: 15 minutes

Ingredients:

- 3 cups russet potato, chopped
- 1 teaspoon salt
- 1 tablespoon butter
- 1 oz fresh dill, chopped
- 3 cups of water

Directions:

1. Boil potatoes in water for 15 minutes or until it is soft.
2. Then drain the water and mash the potato with the help of the potato masher.
3. Add dill, butter, and salt.
4. Mix the meal.

per serving: 136 calories, 3g protein, 31.1g carbohydrates, 0.3g fat, 5g fiber, 0mg cholesterol, 641mg sodium, 716mg potassium

Green Cabbage Coleslaw

Yield: 4 servings | **Prep time:** 10 minutes
Cook time: 0 minutes

Ingredients:

- 2 cups green cabbage, shredded
- 1 apple, chopped
- ¼ cup fresh parsley, chopped
- ¼ cup plain yogurt
- 1 teaspoon garlic, minced

Directions:

1. Mix green cabbage with apple, and parsley.
2. Then add raisins, minced garlic, and plain yogurt.
3. Mix the coleslaw.

per serving: 62 calories, 1.7g protein, 14.1g carbohydrates, 0.3g fat, 2.7g fiber, 1mg cholesterol, 28mg sodium, 221mg potassium

Butter Snap Peas

Yield: 2 servings | **Prep time:** 10 minutes
Cook time: 4 minutes

Ingredients:

- ½ cup snap peas, cooked
- 1 tablespoon butter
- 1 tablespoon hot sauce
- 1 teaspoon olive oil
- 1 oz fresh cilantro, chopped

Directions:

1. Mix snap peas and butter in the saucepan and cook for 4 minutes.
2. Then add cilantro, olive oil, and hot sauce.
3. Stir the meal with the help of a spoon.

per serving: 106 calories, 5.5g protein, 18g carbohydrates, 3.2g fat, 4.6g fiber, 0mg cholesterol, 223mg sodium, 682mg potassium

Paprika Avocado Bites

Yield: 4 servings | **Prep time:** 10 minutes
Cook time: 0 minutes

Ingredients:

- 1 avocado, pitted, cubed
- 1 teaspoon smoked paprika
- 1 tablespoon avocado oil
- ¼ teaspoon dried rosemary
- ¼ teaspoon dried cilantro

Directions:

1. Put the smoked paprika and olive oil in the shallow bowl.
2. Add dried rosemary and dried cilantro.

3. Stir the mixture.
4. Sprinkle the avocado with the paprika mixture.
5. Stir the meal gently.

per serving: 134 calories, 1g protein, 4.7g carbohydrates, 13.3g fat, 3.5g fiber, 0mg cholesterol, 3mg sodium, 251mg potassium

Fast Tomatoes Salad

Yield: 4 servings | **Prep time:** 10 minutes
Cook time: 0 minutes

Ingredients:

- 1 cups heirloom tomatoes, sliced
- 1 cup arugula, chopped
- 1 red onion, chopped
- 1 teaspoon salt
- 2 tablespoons olive oil

Directions:

1. Mix tomatoes with arugula, onion, and salt.
2. Then sprinkle the salad with olive oil and stir.

per serving: 166 calories, 4.7g protein, 6g carbohydrates, 14.4g fat, 1g fiber, 22mg cholesterol, 295mg sodium, 75mg potassium

Cucumbers and Bocconcini Bowl

Yield: 4 servings | **Prep time:** 10 minutes
Cook time: 0 minutes

Ingredients:

- 1 cup lettuce, chopped
- 4 oz baby bocconcini
- 1 cup cucumbers, chopped
- 1 teaspoon Plain yogurt
- 2 tablespoons pesto sauce

Directions:

1. Mix cucumbers with spinach.
2. Then sprinkle the mix with pesto sauce and plain yogurt.
3. Transfer the mixture to the serving bowls and top with baby bocconcini.

per serving: 164 calories, 6.3g protein, 3g carbohydrates, 14.7g fat, 0.7g fiber, 17mg cholesterol, 189mg sodium, 101mg potassium

FISH & SEAFOOD

Fish and Seafood

Salmon Tacos

Yield: 4 servings | **Prep time:** 15 minutes
Cook time: 0 minutes

Ingredients:

- 4 pitas
- 7 oz salmon, boiled
- ½ teaspoon cayenne pepper
- ¼ cup green peas, boiled
- 3 tablespoons plain yogurt

Directions:

1. Shred the salmon and mix it with cayenne pepper, green peas, and plain yogurt.
2. Then fill the pittas with salmon mixture and roll them into tacos.

per serving: 274 calories, 19.6g protein, 36.2g carbohydrates, 5g fat, 1.6g fiber, 16mg cholesterol, 356mg sodium, 295mg potassium.

Coriander Seabass

Yield: 2 servings | **Prep time:** 15 minutes
Cook time: 12 minutes

Ingredients:

- 1-pound seabass
- 1 tablespoon ground coriander
- 3 tablespoons avocado oil
- 1 tablespoon lemon juice

Directions:

1. Peel and trim the seabass.
2. Then rub the fish with avocado oil, lemon juice, and ground coriander.
3. Grill the seabass at 400F for 6 minutes per side.

per serving: 301 calories, 0.2g protein, 4g carbohydrates, 24.2g fat, 0.5g fiber, 0mg cholesterol, 227mg sodium, 20mg potassium.

Tilapia Skewers

Yield: 4 servings | **Prep time:** 10 minutes
Cook time: 6 minutes

Ingredients:

- 12 oz tilapia fillet, cubed
- 1 teaspoon plain yogurt
- 1 teaspoon dried rosemary
- 1 teaspoon olive oil
- ½ teaspoon salt

Directions:

1. In the shallow bowl mix salt, olive oil, dried rosemary, and plain yogurt.
2. Then mix plain yogurt mixture with tilapia fillet cubes.
3. String the fillet cubes in the skewers and grill at 385F for 3 minutes per side.

per serving: 123 calories, 16.6g protein, 0.1g carbohydrates, 6.4g fat, 0g fiber, 38mg cholesterol, 329mg sodium, 330mg potassium.

Lime Squid Rings

Yield: 4 servings | **Prep time:** 10 minutes
Cook time: 7 minutes

Ingredients:

- 1-pound squid, sliced
- 1 teaspoon sesame seeds
- 1 tablespoon olive oil
- ½ teaspoon lime zest, grated

Directions:

1. Preheat the olive oil in the skillet.
2. Add lime zest and sesame seeds.
3. Bring the liquid to a boil.
4. Add sliced squid and cook it for 7 minutes.

per serving: 138 calories, 17.8g protein, 4.1g carbohydrates, 5.1g fat, 0.1g fiber, 265mg cholesterol, 51mg sodium, 289mg potassium.

Cod Herbs de Province

Yield: 4 servings | **Prep time:** 15 minutes
Cook time: 40 minutes

Ingredients:

- 15 oz cod fillet
- 1 tablespoon herbs de province
- 2 tablespoons olive oil
- ½ teaspoon salt

Directions:

1. Rub the cod with salt and herbs de province. Leave the fish for 10 minutes to marinate.
2. Then brush it with olive oil and wrap it in foil.
3. Bake the salmon for 40 minutes at 375F.

per serving: 150 calories, 20.7g protein, 0.4g carbohydrates, 7.5g fat, 0.3g fiber, 47mg cholesterol, 338mg sodium, 430mg potassium.

Turmeric Swordfish

Yield: 2 servings | **Prep time:** 10 minutes
Cook time: 10 minutes

Ingredients:

- 2 swordfish fillets
- 1 teaspoon ground turmeric

½ teaspoon salt
1 tablespoon olive oil

Directions:

1. Sprinkle the fish fillet with ground turmeric and salt from each side.
2. Preheat the olive oil well and put the swordfish fillets in it.
3. Fry the fillets for 4 minutes per side or until they are light brown.

per serving: 177 calories, 27.2g protein, 1g carbohydrates, 5.5g fat, 0.7g fiber, 53mg cholesterol, 704mg sodium, 438mg potassium.

Cumin Shrimps

Yield: 3 servings | **Prep time:** 10 minutes
Cook time: 5 minutes

Ingredients:

- 1 teaspoon ground cumin
- 1-pound shrimp, peeled
- Cooking spray

Directions:

1. Mix shrimp with ground cumin and transfer in the skillet. Spray them with cooking spray.
2. Cook the shrimp for 2 minutes and then flip on another side.
3. Cook the shrimp for 1 minute more.

per serving: 180 calories, 34.4g protein, 2.3g carbohydrates, 2.6g fat, 0g fiber, 318mg cholesterol, 369mg sodium, 257mg potassium.

Salmon Coated in Cheese

Yield: 2 servings | **Prep time:** 10 minutes
Cook time: 18 minutes

Ingredients:

- 10 oz tilapia fillet
- 2 oz basil, chopped
- 1 tablespoon olive oil
- 2 oz Provolone cheese, shredded

Directions:

1. Mix olive oil and basil.
2. Brush the fish with the basil mixture and put it in the tray.
3. Top it with Provolone cheese and bake in the preheated 375F oven for 18 minutes.

per serving: 298 calories, 34.9g protein, 1.4g carbohydrates, 17.2g fat, 0.3g fiber, 103mg cholesterol, 321mg sodium, 28mg potassium.

Salmon in Lemon Marinade

Yield: 4 servings | **Prep time:** 20 minutes
Cook time: 4 minutes

Ingredients:

- 16 oz salmon fillet, cubed
- ¼ cup lemon juice
- 1 teaspoon Erythritol
- 1 tablespoon olive oil
- ½ teaspoon dried basil

Directions:

1. Mix lemon juice with Erythritol, olive oil, and dried basil.
2. Then put the salmon cubes in the lemon marinade and marinate for 15 minutes in the fridge.
3. Then grill the fish at 400F for 2 minutes per side.

per serving: 200 calories, 22.2g protein, 4.8g carbohydrates, 10.6g fat, 0.1g fiber, 50mg cholesterol, 50mg sodium, 500mg potassium.

Yogurt Cod

Yield: 3 servings | **Prep time:** 10 minutes
Cook time: 10 minutes

Ingredients:

- 3 cod fillets
- 3 tablespoons yogurt
- 1 teaspoon dried rosemary
- ½ teaspoon salt

Directions:

1. Sprinkle the cod fillets with dried rosemary and salt. Mix it with yogurt.
2. Cook the fish for 5 minutes from each side on low heat.

per serving: 197 calories, 21.2g protein, 0.5g carbohydrates, 12.6g fat, 0.2g fiber, 86mg cholesterol, 122mg sodium, 12mg potassium.

Cod with Applesauce

Yield: 4 servings | **Prep time:** 10 minutes
Cook time: 15 minutes

Ingredients:

- 1-pound cod fillet
- ½ cup applesauce
- ½ teaspoon dried basil
- 1 teaspoon whole-grain flour
- ½ teaspoon chili powder
- 1 teaspoon olive oil

Directions:

1. Chop the cod fillet roughly and roast with olive oil

for 2 minutes per side.

2. Then mix applesauce with dried basil, flour, and chili powder.
3. Pour the liquid over the fish and close the lid.
4. Simmer the fish for 10 minutes on low heat.

per serving: 123 calories, 20.4g protein, 5.3g carbohydrates, 2.3g fat, 0.2g fiber, 56mg cholesterol, 76mg sodium, 85mg potassium.

Stuffed Tilapia

Yield: 3 servings | **Prep time:** 15 minutes
Cook time: 30 minutes

Ingredients:

- 10 oz tilapia, trimmed
- 3 oz white beans, canned
- 1 tablespoon olive oil
- ¼ teaspoon sesame seeds
- ½ teaspoon white pepper
- ½ teaspoon ground turmeric

Directions:

1. Mix ground turmeric, white pepper, and sesame seeds.
2. Rub the fish with spices and brush with olive oil.
3. Then fill the fish with white beans and secure it with toothpicks.
4. Wrap the tilapia in the foil and bake at 400F for 30 minutes.

per serving: 231 calories, 24g protein, 17.9g carbohydrates, 7.1g fat, 4.5g fiber, 38mg cholesterol, 66mg sodium, 400mg potassium.

Sheet-Pan Tilapia

Yield: 3 servings | **Prep time:** 10 minutes
Cook time: 40 minutes

Ingredients:

- 15 oz tilapia, trimmed, chopped
- 1 bell pepper, roughly chopped
- 1 chili pepper, chopped
- 1 teaspoon allspices
- 2 tablespoons olive oil

Directions:

1. Line the baking tray with baking paper.
2. Put fish, bell pepper, and chili pepper on the tray.
3. Sprinkle the ingredients with all spices and olive oil. Gently stir them.
4. Bake the meal at 375F for 40 minutes.

per serving: 282 calories, 0.6g protein, 9.1g carbohydrates, 14.3g fat, 0.9g fiber, 0mg cholesterol, 363mg sodium, 130mg potassium.

Seabass Puttanesca

Yield: 2 servings | **Prep time:** 10 minutes
Cook time: 20 minutes

Ingredients:

- ½ teaspoon mustard
- 1 tablespoon avocado oil
- 2 oz onion, diced
- ¼ teaspoon garlic powder
- 1 tomato, chopped
- 3 kalamata olives, sliced
- 1 teaspoon fresh cilantro, chopped
- 8 oz seabass fillet
- ¼ cup of water

Directions:

1. Heat the oil in the skillet and add fish fillets. Roast them for 3 minutes per side.
2. Remove the fillets from the skillet.
3. Add all remaining ingredients to the skillet and roast them for 10 minutes.
4. Then stir well and add fish.
5. Close the lid and cook the meal for 7 minutes more.

per serving: 180 calories, 21.9g protein, 4.1g carbohydrates, 9g fat, 1.1g fiber, 55mg cholesterol, 102mg sodium, 79mg potassium.

Tilapia under Delightful Gravy

Yield: 4 servings | **Prep time:** 15 minutes
Cook time: 15 minutes

Ingredients:

- 15 oz tilapia fillet, chopped
- 3 walnuts, grinded
- ½ cup cream cheese
- 1 teaspoon dried thyme
- ½ teaspoon dried sage
- ¼ cup Cheddar cheese, shredded

Directions:

1. Bring the cream cheese to a boil and add thyme and sage.
2. Add ground walnuts and tilapia.
3. Simmer the meal for 10 minutes on medium heat.
4. Then add cheddar cheese, gently stir the ingredients and close the lid.
5. Cook it for 5 minutes or until the cheese is dissolved.
6. Serve the fish with cheese gravy.

per serving: 175 calories, 15.9g protein, 1.8g carbohydrates, 12.1g fat, 0.8g fiber, 40mg cholesterol, 67mg sodium, 315mg potassium.

Pepper Fish

Yield: 2 servings | Prep time: 10 minutes
Cook time: 25 minutes

Ingredients:

- 7 oz halibut, chopped
- ½ cup sweet pepper, chopped
- 1 white onion, diced
- 1 tablespoon olive oil
- 1 tablespoon avocado oil
- ½ teaspoon lemon juice

Directions:

1. Heat avocado oil in the skillet.
2. Add chopped halibut and cook it for 2 minutes per side on high heat.
3. Then add white onion, olive oil, lemon juice, and tomatoes.
4. Sauté fish for 15 minutes on medium heat.

per serving: 197 calories,23.8g protein, 4.7g carbohydrates, 9.8g fat, 1.4g fiber, 35mg cholesterol, 54mg sodium, 169mg potassium.

Stuffed Halibut

Yield: 4 servings | Prep time: 15 minutes
Cook time: 30 minutes

Ingredients:

- 1 tablespoon capers, drained
- 1-pound halibut fillet
- ½ teaspoon smoked paprika
- 1 tablespoon lime juice
- 1 tablespoon olive oil
- ½ teaspoon chili powder

Directions:

1. Place the capers on the halibut fillet.
2. Then roll it and secure it with toothpicks.
3. Gently rub the stuffed fish with smoked paprika, lime juice, olive oil, and chili powder.
4. Put the stuffed mackerel in the tray and bake at 375F for 30 minutes.
5. Then remove the toothpicks and slice the fish into servings.

per serving: 330 calories, 27.2g protein, 0.5g carbohydrates, 23.8g fat, 0.3g fiber, 85mg cholesterol, 162mg sodium, 473mg potassium.

Baked Mackerel with Goat Cheese

Yield: 6 servings | Prep time: 10 minutes
Cook time: 40 minutes

Ingredients:

- 12 oz mackerel fillet, roughly chopped
- 1 teaspoon allspices
- 1 tablespoon olive oil
- ½ teaspoon dried rosemary
- 5 oz Goat cheese, crumbled

Directions:

1. Sprinkle the mackerel fillet cubes with allspices, dried rosemary, and olive oil.
2. Then line the baking tray with baking paper and put the fish inside. Flatten it in one layer.
3. Top the mackerel with crumbled Goat cheese and cook at 365F for 40 minutes.

per serving: 289 calories, 15.3g protein, 1.3g carbohydrates, 25g fat, 0.1g fiber, 21mg cholesterol, 264mg sodium, 19mg potassium.

Cod and Orange Skewers

Yield: 6 servings | Prep time: 15 minutes
Cook time: 6 minutes

Ingredients:

- 1-pound cod, cubed
- 1 tablespoon plain yogurt
- 1 teaspoon ground thyme
- ½ teaspoon chili powder
- 2 orange, peeled, cubed

Directions:

1. In the mixing bowl, mix plain yogurt, ground thyme, and chili powder.
2. Then rub every cod cube in the plain yogurt mixture.
3. After this, string the cod and orange into the skewers and grill at 400F for 3 minutes per side or until the fish and orange are light brown.

per serving: 117 calories, 15g protein, 4.1g carbohydrates, 4.8g fat, 0.5g fiber, 33mg cholesterol, 38mg sodium, 333mg potassium.

Za'atar Mackerel

Yield: 2 servings | Prep time: 10 minutes
Cook time: 9 minutes

Ingredients:

- 8 oz mackerel fillet
- 1 teaspoon za'atar
- 1 tablespoon lemon juice
- 1 tablespoon olive oil

Directions:

1. Preheat the olive oil in the skillet and add za'atar. Roast it for 1 minute.
2. Cook the mixture for 20 seconds.
3. Remove za'atar from the skillet.
4. Put the mackerel fillets in the fragrant olive oil and

cook for 3 minutes from both sides.

5. Sprinkle the cooked fish with lemon juice.

per serving: 154 calories, 121.2g protein, 0.5g carbohydrates, 7.8g fat, 0g fiber, 55mg cholesterol, 40mg sodium, 6mg potassium.

Smoked Paprika Squid Tubes

Yield: 2 servings | **Prep time:** 15 minutes
Cook time: 8 minutes

Ingredients:

- 2 squid tubes, trimmed
- 1 teaspoon tomato paste
- 1 teaspoon smoked paprika
- 1 tablespoon plain yogurt
- 1 tablespoon olive oil
- 1 teaspoon ground cumin

Directions:

1. Mix garlic with tomato paste, smoked paprika, ground cumin, and plain yogurt.
2. Then gently rub every squid tube with cumin mixture and leave for 10-15 minutes to marinate.
3. After this, heat the olive oil in the skillet.
4. Add squid tubes and cook for 4 minutes on low heat.
5. Flip the squid tubes to another side and cook for 2 minutes more.

per serving: 134 calories, 12.7g protein, 2.2g carbohydrates, 8.7g fat, 0.4g fiber, 350mg cholesterol, 549mg sodium, 78mg potassium.

Braised Mackerel

Yield: 4 servings | **Prep time:** 10 minutes
Cook time: 17 minutes

Ingredients:

- 16 oz mackerel fillet
- ½ cup of water
- 1 teaspoon ground coriander
- 1 teaspoon olive oil
- ½ teaspoon chili flakes

Directions:

1. Chop the mackerel and put it in the saucepan.
2. Add olive oil and roast the mackerel for 30 seconds from each side.
3. Add chili flakes, water, and ground coriander.
4. Close the lid and braise the fish for 10-15 minutes on low heat.

per serving: 163 calories, 22g protein, 0.3g carbohydrates, 8.4g fat, 0.1g fiber, 50mg cholesterol, 51mg sodium, 438mg potassium.

Za'atar Shrimps

Yield: 4 servings | **Prep time:** 10 minutes
Cook time: 5 minutes

Ingredients:

- 12 oz shrimp, peeled
- 1 tablespoon za'atar spices
- 1 tablespoon olive oil

Directions:

1. Mix za'atar spices with olive oil.
2. Sprinkle the shrimp with this mixture.
3. After this, preheat the skillet well.
4. Put the shrimp in the hot skillet in one layer and cook for 1 minute from each side.

per serving: 164 calories, 19.4g protein, 1.5g carbohydrates, 8.5g fat, 0.1g fiber, 179mg cholesterol, 355mg sodium, 146mg potassium.

Salmon Pie

Yield: 8 servings | **Prep time:** 15 minutes
Cook time: 30 minutes

Ingredients:

- 8 oz puff pastry
- 7 oz salmon, boiled
- 1 oz fresh cilantro, chopped
- 1 apple, chopped
- 1 teaspoon olive oil
- 3 tablespoons cream cheese

Directions:

1. Shred the salmon and mix it with cilantro, apple, and cream cheese.
2. Roll up the puff pastry and put it in the pie mold.
3. Put the salmon mixture in the puff pastry, flatten it and sprinkle it with olive oil.
4. Bake the pie for 30 minutes at 365F.

per serving: 234 calories, 9.5g protein, 18.8g carbohydrates, 13.8g fat, 1.6g fiber, 9mg cholesterol, 92mg sodium, 249mg potassium.

Seabass in Coconut Gravy

Yield: 4 servings | **Prep time:** 10 minutes
Cook time: 25 minutes

Ingredients:

- 4 seabass fillets, chopped
- ¼ cup coconut cream
- 1 tablespoon whole-grain flour
- 1 teaspoon ground black pepper
- ½ teaspoon dried oregano

Directions:

1. Mix coconut cream with flour. Add ground black pepper and dried oregano.
2. Bring the coconut cream mixture to a boil, and add a chopped seabass fillet.
3. Carefully coat the fish in the cream mixture and bake in the oven at 365F for 20 minutes.

per serving: 163 calories, 29.5g protein, 2.3g carbohydrates, 4.1g fat, 0.5g fiber, 48mg cholesterol, 31mg sodium, 653mg potassium.

Thyme Swordfish

Yield: 2 servings | Prep time: 10 minutes
Cook time: 5 minutes

Ingredients:

- 9 oz swordfish fillet
- 1 teaspoon dried thyme
- 1 teaspoon canola oil

Directions:

1. Cut the fish into 2 servings and rub with thyme.
2. Sprinkle the fillets with canola oil.
3. After this, preheat the grill to 390F.
4. Put the swordfish fillets on the hot grill and cook for 2.5 minutes from each side.

per serving: 203 calories, 32.5g protein, 0.5g carbohydrates, 7g fat, 0.4g fiber, 64mg cholesterol, 147mg sodium, 484mg potassium.

Blackened Tuna

Yield: 4 servings | Prep time: 10 minutes
Cook time: 20 minutes

Ingredients:

- 1-pound tuna fillet
- 2 tablespoons canola oil
- ½ teaspoon chili flakes
- ½ teaspoon ground nutmeg
- ½ teaspoon ground cumin

Directions:

1. Mix chili flakes, ground nutmeg, and ground cumin.
2. Rub the tuna fillet with the spice mixture and sprinkle with canola oil.
3. Put the tuna fillet in the tray and bake at 365F for 20 minutes.
4. Then cut the tuna fillet into servings.

per serving: 154 calories, 20.3g protein, 0.3g carbohydrates, 8.2g fat, 0.1g fiber, 56mg cholesterol, 71mg sodium, 6mg potassium.

Chili Lobster Tails

Yield: 4 servings | Prep time: 10 minutes
Cook time: 55 minutes

Ingredients:

- 4 lobster tails
- ½ teaspoon salt
- ½ teaspoon chili powder
- 1 cup water
- 4 teaspoons butter

Directions:

1. Pour water into the pan, add salt, and add lobster tails.
2. Boil the lobster tails for 15 minutes.
3. Then transfer the lobster tails to the serving plates, sprinkle with chili powder, and top with butter.

per serving: 79 calories, 12.7g protein, 0.2g carbohydrates, 2.7g fat, 0.1g fiber, 40mg cholesterol, 331mg sodium, 98mg potassium

Pan-Fried Shrimps

Yield: 2 servings | Prep time: 10 minutes
Cook time: 5 minutes

Ingredients:

- 13 oz shrimp, peeled
- ¼ teaspoon dried oregano
- ½ teaspoon minced garlic
- 1 tablespoon olive oil

Directions:

1. Mix shrimp with dried oregano and minced garlic.
2. Heat olive oil, add shrimp, and fry them for 1.5 minutes per side.

per serving: 137 calories, 16.2g protein, 0.2g carbohydrates, 7.5g fat, 0g fiber, 124mg cholesterol, 413mg sodium, 199mg potassium.

Seared Halibut

Yield: 2 servings | Prep time: 10 minutes
Cook time: 5 minutes

Ingredients:

- 8 oz halibut fillet
- 1/3 teaspoon salt
- ¼ teaspoon ground nutmeg
- 1 tablespoon avocado oil

Directions:

1. Cut the halibut fillet into 2 fillets and sprinkle with salt and ground nutmeg from both sides.
2. Preheat avocado oil until shimmering.
3. Put halibut in the hot oil and roast for 2 minutes.

4. Then flip the fish to another side and cook for 2 minutes more.

per serving: 321 calories, 27.4g protein, 3.4g carbohydrates, 21.3g fat, 0.6g fiber, 85mg cholesterol, 482mg sodium, 496mg potassium.

Tilapia Tapas

Yield: 2 servings | **Prep time:** 10 minutes
Cook time: 2 minutes

Ingredients:

- 2 oz cheddar cheese, shredded
- 4 oz tilapia fillet, grilled, shredded

Directions:

1. Make 2 rounds in the skillet from cheddar cheese and cook them until the cheese is melted.
2. Then cool the cheese rounds.
3. Put the shredded tilapia on the cheese rounds and roll them.

per serving: 189 calories, 18.1g protein, 0.4g carbohydrates, 12.9g fat, 0g fiber, 55mg cholesterol, 201mg sodium, 246mg potassium.

POULTRY & MEAT

Poultry and Meat

Chicken Breast and Pepper Skillet

Yield: 4 servings | **Prep time:** 10 minutes
Cook time: 23 minutes

Ingredients:

- 1-pound chicken breast, skinless, boneless
- ½ cup bell pepper, chopped
- ½ cup water
- 1 tablespoon tomato paste
- 1 tablespoon olive oil
- 1 teaspoon ground black pepper

Directions:

1. Heat olive oil.
2. Chop the chicken breast and mix with ground black pepper.
3. Put the chicken in the hot oil and roast for 5 minutes.
4. Then stir well and add tomato paste, water, and bell pepper.
5. Close the lid and cook the meal for 15 minutes on medium heat.

per serving: 173 calories, 24.7g protein, 3.2g carbohydrates, 6.5g fat, 0.9g fiber, 73mg cholesterol, 61mg sodium, 561mg potassium

Cheddar Chicken

Yield: 4 servings | **Prep time:** 10 minutes
Cook time: 25 minutes

Ingredients:

- 10 oz chicken breast, skinless, boneless, roughly chopped
- 1 tablespoon avocado oil
- ½ cup coconut milk
- 2 oz Cheddar cheese, grated
- ½ teaspoon chili flakes
- ¼ teaspoon ground nutmeg

Directions:

1. Heat the avocado oil, add chicken breast, and sprinkle with chili flakes.
2. Roast the chicken for 3 minutes and stir.
3. Then add coconut milk, ground nutmeg, and Cheddar cheese.
4. Close the lid and simmer the chicken for 20 minutes on low heat.

per serving: 165 calories, 19.7g protein, 1.6g carbohydrates, 8.7g fat, 0g fiber, 55mg cholesterol, 185mg sodium, 263mg potassium

Italian Style Chicken

Yield: 3 servings | **Prep time:** 15 minutes
Cook time: 30 minutes

Ingredients:

- 1-pound chicken breast, skinless, boneless, chopped
- 1 teaspoon butter
- 1 teaspoon dried oregano
- 1 egg, beaten
- 1 teaspoon ground paprika

Directions:

1. Sprinkle the chopped chicken with dried oregano, egg, and paprika.
2. Mix the chicken well and arrange it in the tray in one layer.
3. Then top the chicken with butter and bake at 360F for 30 minutes.

per serving: 314 calories, 41.1g protein, 1g carbohydrates, 15.2g fat, 0.3g fiber, 182mg cholesterol, 274mg sodium, 624mg potassium

Basil Chicken

Yield: 2 servings | **Prep time:** 10 minutes
Cook time: 30 minutes

Ingredients:

- 8 oz chicken breast, skinless, boneless
- 1 oz fresh basil, chopped
- 1 tablespoon olive oil

Directions:

1. Mix basil with olive oil.
2. Coat the chicken breast in basil mixture and wrap it in foil.
3. Bake the chicken for 30 minutes at 360F.
4. Then slice the chicken into servings.

per serving: 231 calories, 26.3g protein, 1.5g carbohydrates, 12.6g fat, 0.4g fiber, 78mg cholesterol, 200mg sodium, 420mg potassium

Chicken Kebab

Yield: 4 servings | **Prep time:** 15 minutes
Cook time: 17 minutes

Ingredients:

- 1-pound chicken breast, skinless, boneless
- 2 tablespoons plain yogurt
- ½ white onion, grated
- ½ teaspoon salt
- ½ teaspoon chili powder
- 1 teaspoon olive oil

Directions:

1. Cut the chicken breast into cubes.
2. In the mixing bowl, mix plain yogurt, onion, salt, chili powder, and olive oil.
3. Coat every chicken cube in the yogurt mixture.
4. String the chicken into skewers and bake in the preheated to 400F oven for 17 minutes.

per serving: 148 calories, 24.7g protein, 1.4g carbohydrates, 4.1g fat, 0.2g fiber, 73mg cholesterol, 358mg sodium, 479mg potassium

Honey Chicken Wings

Yield: 6 servings | **Prep time:** 10 minutes
Cook time: 10 minutes

Ingredients:

- 6 chicken wings, boneless
- 1 tablespoon honey
- ¼ teaspoon dried thyme
- 2 tablespoons water
- 1 teaspoon avocado oil

Directions:

1. Make the sweet sauce: mix avocado oil, water, dried thyme, and honey.
2. Then preheat the grill to 400F.
3. Brush every chicken wing with honey sauce and put it on the grill.
4. Cook the chicken wings for 5 minutes per side.

per serving: 213 calories, 13.1g protein, 22.1g carbohydrates, 9.2g fat, 0.1g fiber, 20mg cholesterol, 741mg sodium, 12mg potassium

Jalapeno Chicken Thighs

Yield: 4 servings | **Prep time:** 10 minutes
Cook time: 40 minutes

Ingredients:

- 1 tablespoon smoked paprika
- 4 chicken thighs, skinless, boneless
- 2 tablespoons avocado oil
- 1 jalapeno pepper, diced

Directions:

1. Preheat the oven to 365F.
2. Then mix smoked paprika with avocado oil and jalapeno pepper.
3. Then carefully rub the chicken thighs with pepper mixture and bake in the prepared oven for 40 minutes.

per serving: 291 calories, 42.5g protein, 1.2g carbohydrates, 11.8g fat, 0.5g fiber, 130mg cholesterol, 126mg sodium, 391mg potassium

Chicken and Pepper Tray

Yield: 4 servings | **Prep time:** 10 minutes
Cook time: 45 minutes

Ingredients:

- 1 cup bell pepper, roughly chopped
- ½ teaspoon ground black pepper
- 2 tablespoons olive oil
- ½ teaspoon chili flakes
- 4 chicken drumsticks

Directions:

1. Line the baking tray with baking paper.
2. Then sprinkle the chicken drumsticks with chili flakes.
3. After this, put the chicken drumsticks in the tray and top them with bell peppers.
4. Sprinkle the ingredients with ground black pepper and olive oil.
5. Bake the meal at 365F for 45 minutes.

per serving: 161 calories, 13.6g protein, 5.5g carbohydrates, 9.6g fat, 2.3g fiber, 40mg cholesterol, 74mg sodium, 393mg potassium

Lime Chicken

Yield: 6 servings | **Prep time:** 10 minutes
Cook time: 50 minutes

Ingredients:

- 6 chicken thighs, skinless, boneless
- ½ lime, sliced
- ¼ cup plain yogurt
- 1 teaspoon dried basil
- ½ teaspoon salt

Directions:

1. Mix salt with plain yogurt, and dried basil.
2. After this, mix the plain yogurt mixture with the chicken thighs and put it in the baking mold.
3. Top the chicken with sliced lime and cover the mold with foil.
4. Bake the chicken for 50 minutes at 385F.

per serving: 287 calories, 42.9g protein, 1.3g carbohydrates, 11g fat, 0.2g fiber, 131mg cholesterol, 327mg sodium, 387mg potassium

Nutmeg Chicken Drumsticks

Yield: 4 servings | **Prep time:** 10 minutes
Cook time: 20 minutes

Ingredients:

- 4 chicken drumsticks
- 1 tablespoon ground nutmeg
- ¼ teaspoon chili powder

- 2 tablespoons olive oil

Directions:

1. Preheat the olive oil in the skillet until shimmering.
2. Then sprinkle the drumsticks with chili powder and ground nutmeg.
3. Put the chicken drumsticks in the hot olive oil and cook on medium heat for 10 minutes.
4. After this, flip the chicken drumsticks to another side and cook for 8 minutes more.

per serving: 148 calories,12.7g protein, 0.5g carbohydrates, 10.5g fat, 0g fiber, 43mg cholesterol, 38mg sodium, 95mg potassium

Braised Chicken with Corn Kernels

Yield: 4 servings | **Prep time:** 20 minutes
Cook time: 50 minutes

Ingredients:

- 12 oz chicken breast, skinless, boneless, chopped
- ½ cup corn kernels, frozen
- 1 carrot, chopped
- ½ teaspoon cayenne pepper
- 2 cups of water
- 1 teaspoon dried cilantro

Directions:

1. Put all ingredients in the saucepan and close the lid.
2. Braise the chicken for 50 minutes on low heat.
3. After this, leave the cooked meal for 10-15 minutes to rest.

per serving: 120 calories, 19.2g protein, 4.5g carbohydrates, 2.3g fat, 1.5g fiber, 54mg cholesterol, 59mg sodium, 421mg potassium

Coriander Chicken

Yield: 14 servings | **Prep time:** 20 minutes
Cook time: 85 minutes

Ingredients:

- 4-pounds whole chicken
- 2 tablespoons ground coriander
- 2 tablespoons olive oil
- ½ teaspoon ground turmeric
- ½ teaspoon ground clove
- 4 garlic cloves, peeled, crushed

Directions:

1. Fill the chicken with crushed garlic.
2. After this, carefully rub the whole chicken with ground coriander, olive oil, turmeric, and ground clove.
3. Leave the chicken for 10-15 minutes to marinate.
4. Then place it in the tray and transfer it to the oven.

5. Bake the chicken for 85 minutes at 360F.

per serving: 266 calories, 37.6g protein, 0.6g carbohydrates, 11.7g fat, 0.2g fiber, 115mg cholesterol, 112mg sodium, 325mg potassium

Turmeric Chicken Bites

Yield: 8 servings | **Prep time:** 20 minutes
Cook time: 30 minutes

Ingredients:

- 4 tablespoons flour
- 14 oz chicken fillet
- 1 teaspoon ground turmeric
- ½ teaspoon cayenne pepper
- ¼ teaspoon ground black pepper
- 2 tablespoons Philadelphia cheese

Directions:

1. Mix ground turmeric, cayenne pepper, ground black pepper, and flour in the bowl.
2. Then cut the chicken into cubes (bites) and mix them with Philadelphia cheese.
3. Then carefully coat every chicken bite with flour mixture.
4. Arrange the chicken bites in the tray in one layer and bake at 365F for 30 minutes.

per serving: 115 calories, 14.7g protein, 3.2g carbohydrates, 4.5g fat, 0.4g fiber, 45mg cholesterol, 45mg sodium, 147mg potassium

Beef Casserole

Yield: 4 servings | **Prep time:** 25 minutes
Cook time: 35 minutes

Ingredients:

- 2 zucchinis
- 1 cup beef loin, minced
- 1 cup Cheddar cheese, shredded
- 1 teaspoon sunflower oil
- 1 teaspoon ground black pepper
- ½ cup chicken stock

Directions:

1. In the mixing bowl mix up together minced beef and ground black pepper.
2. Slice the zucchinis roughly.
3. Scoop the pulp from the zucchini and fill it with minced beef mixture.
4. Arrange every zucchini ring in the casserole mold.
5. Top the zucchini rings with cheese and chicken stock.
6. Bake the meal for 35 minutes at 355F.

per serving: 253 calories, 30.1g protein, 3.9g carbohydrates, 12.9g fat, 1.2g fiber, 86mg cholesterol, 304mg sodium, 639mg potassium.

Za'atar Chicken Breast

Yield: 4 servings | **Prep time:** 15 minutes
Cook time: 50 minutes

Ingredients:

- 1-pound chicken breast, skinless, boneless
- 1 tablespoon za'atar seasonings
- 2 tablespoons olive oil
- ¼ cup of apple juice

Directions:

1. Rub the chicken breast with za'atar seasonings and brush with olive oil.
2. Then arrange the chicken breast in the tray.
3. Then pour the apple juice over the chicken breast and transfer it the preheated to a 360F oven.
4. Cook the chicken breast for 50 minutes.

per serving: 196 calories, 24.2g protein, 1.6g carbohydrates, 9.9g fat, 0g fiber, 73mg cholesterol, 95mg sodium, 451mg potassium

Chicken Cakes

Yield: 4 servings | **Prep time:** 10 minutes
Cook time: 10 minutes

Ingredients:

- 9 oz chicken fillet, diced
- 1 egg, beaten
- 2 tablespoons coconut shred, unsweetened
- 1 teaspoon cayenne pepper
- 1 tablespoon olive oil

Directions:

1. Mix diced chicken fillet with egg, coconut shred, and cayenne pepper.
2. Then heat the olive oil in the skillet for 1 minute.
3. Then make the medium cakes from the chicken mixture with the help of the spoon and put in the hot oil.
4. Roast the chicken cakes for 4 minutes per side.

per serving: 160 calories, 20.6g protein, 1.2g carbohydrates, 7.8g fat, 0.6g fiber, 98mg cholesterol, 71mg sodium, 212mg potassium.

Cumin Beef Bites

Yield: 6 servings | **Prep time:** 10 minutes
Cook time: 50 minutes

Ingredients:

- 1-pound beef brisket, sliced
- 1 tablespoon apple cider vinegar
- 2 tablespoons olive oil
- 1 teaspoon smoked paprika
- 1 teaspoon ground cumin
- ½ teaspoon dried basil

Directions:

1. Sprinkle the beef slices with apple cider vinegar, ground cumin, olive oil, smoked paprika, and basil.
2. Wrap the beef in the foil and bake in the oven for 50 minutes at 360F.
3. Remove the meat from the oven and discard the foil.

per serving: 182 calories, 23g protein, 0.2g carbohydrates, 9.3g fat, 0.1g fiber, 68mg cholesterol, 50mg sodium, 315mg potassium.

Thyme Beef Steak

Yield: 2 servings | **Prep time:** 10 minutes
Cook time: 14 minutes

Ingredients:

- 6 oz beef steak (2 servings)
- 1 tablespoon dried thyme
- 1 teaspoon salt
- 1 tablespoon canola oil

Directions:

1. Sprinkle the meat with dried thyme and brush with canola oil.
2. Put the beef steaks in the hot skillet and cook for 7 minutes per side.
3. Then transfer the meat to the plates and sprinkle with salt.

per serving: 225 calories, 26.1g protein, 1.5g carbohydrates, 12.5g fat, 1g fiber, 76mg cholesterol, 1219mg sodium, 380mg potassium.

Garlic Pork Meatloaf

Yield: 4 servings | **Prep time:** 10 minutes
Cook time: 35 minutes

Ingredients:

- 1 cup ground lean pork
- 1 egg, beaten
- 1 teaspoon ground paprika
- 1 oz Cheddar cheese, grated
- 1 teaspoon minced garlic
- 1 teaspoon olive oil

Directions:

1. Mix ground pork with egg, ground paprika, garlic, and Cheddar cheese.
2. Then brush the loaf mold with olive oil from the inside.
3. Put the ground pork mixture in the prepared loaf and cover it with foil.
4. Bake the pork meatloaf for 35 minutes at 365F.
5. Then cool the meatloaf well and discard it from the

mold.

6. Slice the meatloaf.

per serving: 170 calories, 25.6g protein, 0.9g carbohydrates, 6.7g fat, 0.2g fiber, 107mg cholesterol, 129mg sodium, 375mg potassium.

Parsley Meat Mince

Yield: 4 servings | **Prep time:** 10 minutes
Cook time: 20 minutes

Ingredients:

- 1 cup ground beef
- 2 tablespoons cream cheese
- 1 oz fresh parsley, chopped
- 1 garlic clove, diced
- 1 tablespoon olive oil

Directions:

1. Heat olive oil in the skillet.
2. Add ground beef and roast it for 5 minutes.
3. Then sprinkle the meat with parsley, cream cheese, and garlic clove.
4. Stir the ground meat mixture well and cook with the closed lid for 15 minutes.

per serving: 107 calories, 7.1g protein, 2.7g carbohydrates, 7.7g fat, 0.8g fiber, 22mg cholesterol, 27mg sodium, 233mg potassium.

Pork Medallions in Yogurt Gravy

Yield: 2 servings | **Prep time:** 20 minutes
Cook time: 23 minutes

Ingredients:

- 6 oz pork tenderloin
- 1 teaspoon olive oil
- ¼ cup plain yogurt
- 1 teaspoon tomato paste
- ½ teaspoon salt

Directions:

1. Cut the pork tenderloin into 2 servings and roast in the olive oil for 3 minutes per side.
2. Meanwhile, whisk the tomato paste with plain yogurt and salt.
3. Pour the yogurt mixture over the meat, coat it well, and close the lid.
4. Cook the tender medallions for 15 minutes on medium heat.

per serving: 180 calories, 24.1g protein, 2.9g carbohydrates, 7.2g fat, 0g fiber, 64mg cholesterol, 70mg sodium, 430mg potassium.

Pork Pate

Yield: 4 servings | **Prep time:** 15 minutes
Cook time: 40 minutes

Ingredients:

- 1 tablespoon butter
- ½ onion, minced
- 7 oz pork loin, chopped
- 3 tablespoons cream cheese
- 1 teaspoon salt
- 2 cups of water

Directions:

1. Put the meat in the water and simmer for 40 minutes.
2. Then blend the cooked meat and mix with butter and onion.
3. Add cream cheese and salt.
4. Carefully stir the pate.

per serving: 135 calories, 13.9g protein, 2.1g carbohydrates, 7.6g fat, 0.4g fiber, 41mg cholesterol, 34mg sodium, 245mg potassium.

Nutmeg Meatballs

Yield: 4 servings | **Prep time:** 15 minutes
Cook time: 10 minutes

Ingredients:

- 10 oz ground lean pork
- 1 teaspoon ground nutmeg
- ½ teaspoon ground paprika
- 2 tablespoons water
- 1 tablespoon olive oil

Directions:

1. Mix ground pork with ground nutmeg, ground paprika, and water.
2. After this, make the small meatballs.
3. Preheat the olive oil in the skillet.
4. Add the meatballs to the hot oil and roast for 4 minutes per side.

per serving: 133 calories, 18.6g protein, 0.3g carbohydrates, 6g fat, 0.2g fiber, 52mg cholesterol, 41mg sodium, 312mg potassium.

Plain Pork Steak

Yield: 2 servings | **Prep time:** 20 minutes
Cook time: 14 minutes

Ingredients:

- 2 pork steaks
- 1 teaspoon salt
- 1 tablespoon olive oil

Directions:

1. Place the meat in the preheated skillet and sprinkle it with olive oil.
2. Roast the steaks for 6 minutes per side.
3. Then sprinkle the cooked steaks with salt.

per serving: 285 calories, 21.9g protein, 0.9g carbohydrates, 21.2g fat, 0.5g fiber, 81mg cholesterol, 50mg sodium, 294mg potassium.

Zucchini and Meat Skewers

Yield: 4 servings | Prep time: 15 minutes
Cook time: 5 minutes

Ingredients:

- 9 oz beef flank steak
- 1 teaspoon apple cider vinegar
- 1 teaspoon olive oil
- ½ teaspoon salt
- 1 zucchini, roughly chopped

Directions:

1. Cut the beef flank into cubes.
2. Then mix apple cider vinegar, olive oil, and salt.
3. Coat every beef cube and zucchini into the apple cider vinegar mixture and string in the skewers.
4. Preheat the grill to 390F and cook the meat skewers for 7 minutes per side.

per serving: 130 calories, 19.4g protein, 0.2g carbohydrates, 5.2g fat, 0.1g fiber, 57mg cholesterol, 339mg sodium, 266mg potassium.

Sage Meatballs

Yield: 3 servings | Prep time: 15 minutes
Cook time: 10 minutes

Ingredients:

- 6 oz lamb mince
- 1 tablespoon olive oil
- 1 tomato, chopped
- 1 tablespoon fine bulgur
- ½ teaspoon salt
- 1 teaspoon dried sage

Directions:

1. Mix all ingredients except olive oil and make the small meatballs.
2. Preheat the olive oil in the skillet.
3. Then put the lamb balls in the hot oil and roast them for 3.5 minutes per side.

per serving: 144 calories, 9.8g protein, 0.6g carbohydrates, 11.4g fat, 0.2g fiber, 0mg cholesterol, 0mg sodium, 11mg potassium.

Clove Pork Loin

Yield: 5 servings | Prep time: 10 minutes
Cook time: 45 minutes

Ingredients:

- 1-pound pork loin
- 1 tablespoon ground clove
- 1 teaspoon olive oil

Directions:

1. Preheat the oven to 375F.
2. Then sprinkle the pork loin with ground clove and olive oil.
3. Then wrap the meat in the foil and bake in the oven for 45 minutes.

per serving: 229 calories, 24.8g protein, 0.2g carbohydrates, 13.6g fat, 0.2g fiber, 73mg cholesterol, 56mg sodium, 388mg potassium.

Tender Beef and Tomatoes Stew

Yield: 5 servings | Prep time: 10 minutes
Cook time: 40 minutes

Ingredients:

- 12 oz beef sirloin, chopped
- 1 cup tomatoes, chopped
- 1 teaspoon ground black pepper
- 1 teaspoon salt
- 1 teaspoon dried basil
- 1 tablespoon olive oil
- ½ cup of water

Directions:

1. Roast the beef with olive oil in the saucepan for 2 minutes per side.
2. Then add tomatoes, ground black pepper, salt, basil, and water.
3. Saute the stew for 40 minutes.

per serving: 267 calories, 28.7g protein, 21.3g carbohydrates, 7.4g fat, 5.3g fiber, 61mg cholesterol, 549mg sodium, 919mg potassium.

Rosemary Lamb Chops

Yield: 2 servings | Prep time: 10 minutes
Cook time: 18 minutes

Ingredients:

- 2 lamb chops
- 1 teaspoon dried rosemary
- 1 teaspoon olive oil

Directions:

1. Preheat the olive oil in the skillet.
2. Meanwhile, sprinkle the lamb chops with dried

rosemary.

3. Massage the meat well with the help of the fingertips.
4. Put the lamb chops in the hot oil and cook for 8 minutes per side on low heat.

per serving: 184 calories, 24 g protein, 0.8 g carbohydrates, 8.8g fat, 0.4g fiber, 77mg cholesterol, 78mg sodium, 315mg potassium.

Tarragon Pork Chops

Yield: 4 servings | **Prep time:** 10 minutes
Cook time: 10 minutes

Ingredients:

- 4 pork chops
- ¼ teaspoon dried tarragon
- 1 tablespoon olive oil

Directions:

1. Prehcat the grill to 385F.
2. Then rub the beef chops with dried tarragon.
3. Brush the meat with olive oil.
4. Grill the pork chops for 5 minutes per side.

per serving: 105 calories, 5.7g protein, 0.4g carbohydrates, 8.8g fat, 0.1g fiber, 15mg cholesterol, 106mg sodium, 8mg potassium.

BREAD
& PIZZAS

Bread and Pizzas

Berries Pizza

Yield: 4 servings | **Prep time:** 15 minutes
Cook time: 0 minutes

Ingredients:

- 4 melon slices
- 1 oz raspberries
- 2 oz goat cheese, crumbled
- 1 teaspoon fresh parsley, chopped

Directions:

1. Put the melon slices on the plate in one layer.
2. Then sprinkle them with raspberries, goat cheese, and fresh parsley.

per serving: 69 calories, 4.4g protein, 1.4g carbohydrates, 5.1g fat, 0.2g fiber, 15mg cholesterol, 49mg sodium, 15mg potassium.

Chicken Pizza

Yield: 6 servings | **Prep time:** 25 minutes
Cook time: 15 minutes

Ingredients:

- 4 oz wheat flour, whole grain
- 2 tablespoons olive oil
- ¼ teaspoon baking powder
- 5 oz chicken fillet, boiled
- 2 oz Parmesan cheese, shredded
- 1 tomato, chopped
- 2 oz bell pepper, chopped

Directions:

1. Make the pizza crust: mix wheat flour, olive oil, and baking powder, and knead the dough.
2. Roll it up in the shape of a pizza crust and transfer it to the pizza mold.
3. Then sprinkle it with chopped tomato, shredded chicken, bell pepper, and Parmesan.
4. Bake the pizza at 365F for 15 minutes.

per serving: 184 calories, 11.9g protein, 15.6g carbohydrates, 8.2g fat, 0.6g fiber, 26mg cholesterol, 79mg sodium, 141mg potassium.

Parmesan Pinwheels

Yield: 6 servings | **Prep time:** 20 minutes
Cook time: 25 minutes

Ingredients:

- 1 teaspoon chili flakes
- ½ teaspoon dried dill
- 1 egg, beaten
- 1 teaspoon cream cheese
- 1 oz Parmesan cheese, grated
- 6 oz pizza dough

Directions:

1. Roll up the pizza dough and cut it into 6 squares.
2. Sprinkle the dough with dried dill, cream cheese, and Parmesan cheese.
3. Roll the dough in the shape of pinwheels, brush with beaten egg, and bake in the preheated to 365F oven for 25 minutes or until the pinwheels are light brown.

per serving: 16 calories, 3.8g protein, 12.1g carbohydrates, 11.2g fat, 1g fiber, 33mg cholesterol, 178mg sodium, 33mg potassium.

Beef Pizza

Yield: 4 servings | **Prep time:** 15 minutes
Cook time: 35 minutes

Ingredients:

- 7 oz ground beef
- 1 tomato, sliced
- ½ teaspoon ground black pepper
- 2 egg whites, whisked
- ½ cup Cheddar cheese, shredded
- 1 teaspoon fresh basil, chopped

Directions:

1. Line the baking tray with baking paper. Preheat the oven to 370F.
2. Mix all ingredients except Cheddar in the mixing bowl.
3. Then place the mixture in the tray and flatten it to get a thick layer.
4. Top the pizza with Cheddar cheese and bake in the oven for 35 minutes.
5. Then cut the cooked pizza into servings.

per serving: 113 calories, 18g protein, 0.7g carbohydrates, 3.8g fat, 0.1g fiber, 46mg cholesterol, 72mg sodium, 244mg potassium.

Oregano Pizza

Yield: 6 servings | **Prep time:** 15 minutes
Cook time: 15 minutes

Ingredients:

- 1 oz pumpkin puree
- 3 tablespoons quinoa flour
- ½ teaspoon dried oregano
- 1 cup Swiss cheese, shredded
- 1 chili pepper, diced
- 1 teaspoon olive oil

Directions:

1. Mix pumpkin puree, quinoa flour, and olive oil. Knead the dough.
2. Roll it up in the shape of a pizza crust and transfer it the lined with a baking paper baking tray.
3. Then top the pizza crust with tomato, oregano, and Swiss cheese.
4. Bake the pizza at 365F for 15 minutes.

per serving: 38 calories, 2g protein, 3.3g carbohydrates, 1.8g fat, 0.6g fiber, 3mg cholesterol, 30mg sodium, 36mg potassium.

Fluffy Bread with Olives

Yield: 8 servings | **Prep time:** 25 minutes
Cook time: 65 minutes

Ingredients:

- 1 cup green olives, pitted, sliced
- 1 tablespoon olive oil
- ½ oz fresh yeast
- 4 oz cream cheese
- 2 cup wheat flour, whole grain
- 3 eggs, beaten
- 1 teaspoon butter, melted

Directions:

1. In the big bowl combine fresh yeast and cream cheese. Stir it until the yeast is dissolved.
2. Then add butter and eggs. Stir the dough mixture until homogenous, and add 1 cup of wheat flour. Mix it up until smooth.
3. Add olives and remaining flour. Add olive oil and knead the non-sticky dough.
4. Transfer the dough to the non-sticky dough mold.
5. Cook the bread for 65 minutes at 350 F.
6. When the bread is cooked, cool it well and remove it from the mold.
7. Slice the bread.

per serving: 176 calories, 6.6g protein, 27g carbohydrates, 4.6g fat, 1.8g fiber, 62mg cholesterol, 179mg sodium, 120mg potassium.

Chicken Flatbread

Yield: 8 servings | **Prep time:** 30 minutes
Cook time: 30 minutes

Ingredients:

- 1 ½ cup ground chicken
- 1 teaspoon baking powder
- ¼ cup cream cheese
- 9 oz wheat flour, whole grain
- 1 teaspoon avocado oil
- 1 teaspoon tomato paste

Directions:

1. Make the yeast dough: mix baking powder, cream cheese, and whole-grain flour.
2. Knead the non-sticky dough and leave it in a warm place for 15 minutes.
3. After this, roll up the dough in the shape of a square and transfer it to the lined baking tray.
4. Bake it at 365F for 10 minutes.
5. Meanwhile, mix ground chicken, tomato paste, and avocado oil.
6. Spread the ground chicken mixture over the flatbread and bake it at 365f for 20 minutes more.

per serving: 246 calories, 20.7g protein, 25.8g carbohydrates, 7.3g fat, 0.9g fiber, 64mg cholesterol, 73mg sodium, 291mg potassium.

Parmesan Bites

Yield: 8 servings | **Prep time:** 20 minutes
Cook time: 10 minutes

Ingredients:

- 2 tablespoons butter, softened
- 1/3 cup plain yogurt
- 9 oz wheat flour, whole grain
- 1 teaspoon avocado oil
- 1 cup fresh spinach, chopped
- 1 oz Parmesan, grated

Directions:

1. Mix avocado oil and plain yogurt.
2. Then add flour and knead the soft dough.
3. Cut the dough into 8 pieces and roll it into the rounds.
4. Then preheat the butter in the skillet.
5. Put the dough rounds in the skillet and roast for 3 minutes per side.
6. Then top the cooked dough bites with spinach and Parmesan.
7. Cook the meal with a closed lid for 2 minutes.

per serving: 174 calories, 5.2g protein, 26.3g carbohydrates, 5.2g fat, 1.1g fiber, 3mg cholesterol, 41mg sodium, 86mg potassium.

Spinach Pizza

Yield: 4 servings | **Prep time:** 15 minutes
Cook time: 20 minutes

Ingredients:

- 7 oz pizza crust
- 5 oz fresh spinach, chopped
- 1 teaspoon fresh parsley, chopped
- 1 tomato, sliced
- 1 cup Monterey Jack cheese, shredded

Directions:

1. Line the pizza mold with baking paper.
2. Then put the pizza crust inside.
3. Top it with sliced tomato, spinach, and parsley.
4. Then top the pizza with Monterey Jack cheese and transfer it to the preheated 365F oven.
5. Cook the pizza for 20 minutes.

per serving: 247 calories, 12.1g protein, 28.2g carbohydrates, 10.2g fat, 2.9g fiber, 25mg cholesterol, 544mg sodium, 191mg potassium.

Plain Cheese Pizza

Yield: 6 servings | **Prep time:** 15 minutes
Cook time: 10 minutes

Ingredients:

- 1 pizza crust, cooked
  ½ cup Mozzarella, shredded
- ½ cup Swiss cheese, shredded
- 2 oz Parmesan, grated
- ¼ cup tomato sauce
- 1 teaspoon dried basil

Directions:

1. Put the pizza crust in the baking pan.
2. Then brush it with tomato sauce and dried basil.
3. After this, sprinkle the pizza with Mozzarella, Swiss cheese, and Parmesan.
4. Bake the pizza for 10 minutes at 375F.

per serving: 106 calories, 7g protein, 6.3g carbohydrates, 6.1g fat, 0.3g fiber, 18mg cholesterol, 292mg sodium, 43mg potassium.

Sweet Pizza

Yield: 4 servings | **Prep time:** 10 minutes
Cook time: 10 minutes

Ingredients:

- 5 oz flatbread pizza crust
- 4 oz Feta cheese, crumbled
- 2 oz raisins
- ¼ cup fresh arugula, chopped

Directions:

1. Put the flatbread pizza crust in the baking tray.
2. Then put raisins on the pizza crust.
3. Sprinkle the raisins with crumbled Feta cheese and bake at 400F for 10 minutes.
4. Top the cooked pizza with an arugula.

per serving: 167 calories, 9.1g protein, 9.5g carbohydrates, 10.4g fat, 1.2g fiber, 29mg cholesterol, 341mg sodium, 73mg potassium.

Sprout Pizza

Yield: 6 servings | **Prep time:** 10 minutes
Cook time: 25 minutes

Ingredients:

- 4 tablespoons pizza sauce
- 7 oz pizza dough
- 1 tomato, sliced
- 3 oz bean sprouts
- 5 oz chickpeas, canned
- ½ cup Mozzarella cheese, shredded

Directions:

1. Roll up the pizza dough in the shape of a pizza crust and transfer it to the pizza mold.
2. Then brush the pizza crust with pizza sauce and sprinkle with bean sprouts, tomato, and chickpeas.
3. Top the chickpeas with mozzarella cheese and bake the pizza for 25 minutes at 355F.

per serving: 266 calories, 7.6g protein, 31.9g carbohydrates, 12.4g fat, 6g fiber, 1mg cholesterol, 223mg sodium, 310mg potassium.

Mozzarella Pizza

Yield: 6 servings | **Prep time:** 10 minutes
Cook time: 15 minutes

Ingredients:

- 1 pizza crust
- 1 tablespoon avocado oil
- 1 tablespoon fresh dill
- 1 cup Mozzarella cheese, shredded
- 1 tablespoon fresh basil leaves

Directions:

1. Top the pizza crust with mozzarella, dill, olive oil, and fresh basil.
2. Bake the pizza at 400F for 15 minutes.

per serving: 94 calories, 3.4g protein, 12.7g carbohydrates, 3.5g fat, 0.7g fiber, 3mg cholesterol, 215mg sodium, 72mg potassium.

Goat Cheese Pizza

Yield: 6 servings | **Prep time:** 10 minutes
Cook time: 20 minutes

Ingredients:

- 6 oz pizza dough
- 5 oz hummus
- 3 oz Goat cheese, crumbled
- 1 tablespoon fresh dill, chopped
- ½ cup green olives, sliced
- 3 sun-dried tomatoes, chopped
- 1 tablespoon avocado oil

Directions:

1. Roll up the pizza dough in the shape of the pizza crust.
2. Then place it in a pizza mold and brush it with avocado oil.
3. Spread the pizza crust with hummus and sprinkle with dill, green olives, sun-dried tomatoes, and crumbled goat cheese.
4. Bake the pizza at 400F for 20 minutes.

per serving: 237 calories, 6.2g protein, 19.2g carbohydrates, 15.6g fat, 3.6g fiber, 13mg cholesterol, 485mg sodium, 237mg potassium.

Cheddar Pizza

Yield: 8 servings | Prep time: 15 minutes
Cook time: 25 minutes

Ingredients:

- 6 oz pizza dough
- 1 cup Shiitake mushrooms, chopped
- 1 cup Cheddar cheese, shredded
- 3 oz Feta cheese, crumbled
- 1 tablespoon olive oil
- 1 teaspoon dried thyme
- ½ teaspoon dried basil

Directions:

1. Roll up the pizza dough and put it in the lined with a baking paper baking tray.
2. Then preheat olive oil in the skillet.
3. Add Shiitake mushrooms and cook them for 5 minutes.
4. Then put the mushrooms over the pizza dough.
5. Sprinkle the mushrooms with Cheddar cheese and Feta cheese.
6. Then sprinkle the pizza with thyme and basil.
7. Bake the pizza at 400F for 20 minutes.

per serving: 223 calories,8.2g protein, 9.9g carbohydrates, 16.8g fat, 0.9g fiber, 26mg cholesterol, 228mg sodium, 74mg potassium.

Brie Cheese Pizza

Yield: 6 servings | Prep time: 10 minutes
Cook time: 12 minutes

Ingredients:

- 1 pizza crust
- 2 apples, sliced
- 5 oz brie cheese, crumbled
- 2 tablespoons cream cheese
- ½ teaspoon dried oregano

Directions:

1. Spread the pizza crust with cream cheese.

2. Then put the sliced apples on the pizza crust on one layer and sprinkle with brie cheese and dried oregano.
3. Bake the pizza at 400F for 12 minutes.

per serving: 160 calories, 6.5g protein, 17.3g carbohydrates, 8.2 fat, 3.1g fiber, 26mg cholesterol, 384mg sodium, 85mg potassium.

Garlic Pizza

Yield: 2 servings | Prep time: 5 minutes
Cook time: 15 minutes

Ingredients:

- 2 slices focaccia bread
- 2 tomatoes, sliced
- ½ teaspoon dried basil
- 2 oz Parmesan, sliced
- 1 teaspoon minced garlic
- 1 tablespoon tomato paste

Directions:

1. Spread the bread with tomato paste and minced garlic.
2. Then top the bread slices with Parmesan and tomatoes and sprinkle with dried basil.
3. Bake the pizzas for 5 minutes at 400F.

per serving: 189 calories, 12.1g protein, 22.5g carbohydrates, 6.2g fat, 2.5g fiber, 15mg cholesterol, 344mg sodium, 385 potassium.

Arugula Pizza

Yield: 6 servings | Prep time: 10 minutes
Cook time: 20 minutes

Ingredients:

- 6 oz pizza dough
- 4 tablespoons pesto sauce
- 1 cup arugula
- 1 tablespoon lemon juice

Directions:

1. Line the baking tray with baking paper and put the pizza dough inside.
2. Then brush it with pesto sauce.
3. Bake it for 20 minutes at 400F.
4. Then sprinkle the cooked pizza with arugula and lemon juice.

per serving: 184 calories, 2.9g protein, 13.9g carbohydrates, 13.1g fat, 1.5g fiber, 3mg cholesterol, 203mg sodium, 97mg potassium.

Dates Pizza

Yield: 8 servings | **Prep time:** 15 minutes
Cook time: 20 minutes

Ingredients:

- 8 oz pizza dough
- 4 dates, pitted, chopped
- 1 teaspoon liquid honey
- 1 cup Swiss cheese, shredded
- ½ cup marinara sauce

Directions:

1. Brush the pizza dough with marinara sauce and transfer it to the pizza mold.
2. Then add dates and Swiss cheese.
3. Bake the pizza at 400F for 20 minutes.
4. When the pizza is cooked, sprinkle it with liquid honey.

per serving: 171 calories, 3.1g protein, 18g carbohydrates, 9.8g fat, 1.8g fiber, 2mg cholesterol, 223mg sodium, 99mg potassium.

Tomato Tart

Yield: 6 servings | **Prep time:** 15 minutes
Cook time: 30 minutes

Ingredients:

- 3 tomatoes, sliced
- 1 tablespoon olive oil
- ¼ teaspoon dried thyme
- 5 oz Feta, crumbled
- 1 oz fresh basil
- 5 oz puff pastry

Directions:

1. Put the tomatoes in the tray in one layer and sprinkle with olive oil and dried thyme.
2. Bake the tomatoes for 10 minutes at 400F.
3. Then roll up the puff pastry into the shape of a square.
4. Put the baked tomatoes and Feta over the puff pastry one by one.
5. Then transfer the prepared tart to the oven and cook it for 20 minutes at 385F.

per serving: 229 calories, 9.1g protein, 14.1 carbohydrates, 15.7g fat, 1.2g fiber, 13mg cholesterol, 204mg sodium, 175mg potassium.

Ricotta Cheese Pizza

Yield: 4 servings | **Prep time:** 15 minutes
Cook time: 18 minutes

Ingredients:

- 4 oz pizza dough

- 3 tablespoons ricotta cheese
- ½ cup Cheddar cheese, shredded
- 1 tablespoon olive oil
- 2 tablespoons fresh dill, chopped
- ½ teaspoon minced garlic

Directions:

1. Roll up the pizza dough in the shape of the pizza crust.
2. Then mix minced garlic with olive oil.
3. Brush the pizza crust with garlic oil.
4. Then sprinkle the pizza crust with ricotta and Cheddar cheese.
5. Add fresh dill and transfer the pizza to the preheated 400F oven.
6. Cook the pizza for 18 minutes.

per serving: 190 calories, 4g protein, 12.9g carbohydrates, 13.7g fat, 1g fiber, 5mg cholesterol, 173mg sodium, 37mg potassium.

Olives Pizza

Yield: 8 servings | **Prep time:** 10 minutes
Cook time: 10 minutes

Ingredients:

- 8 whole-grain pitta
- 8 teaspoons marinara sauce
- 8 black olives, sliced
- 6 oz Provolone cheese, grated

Directions:

1. Brush every pita with marinara sauce.
2. Then top them with black olives and grated Provolone cheese.
3. Bake the pita pizzas at 375F for 10 minutes.

per serving: 205 calories, 10.4g protein, 25g carbohydrates, 6.7g fat, 3.2g fiber, 15mg cholesterol, 251mg sodium, 47mg potassium.

Jewish Pita

Yield: 12 servings | **Prep time:** 20 minutes | **Cook time:** 10 minutes

Ingredients:

- 2 cups whole-grain flour
- 1 cup water, warm
- 1 teaspoon dried yeast
- ¼ teaspoon salt
- 3 tablespoons avocado oil
- ½ teaspoon dried dill

Directions:

1. Mix water and dried yeast. Stir the ingredients until the yeast is dissolved.

2. Then add flour and stir until the mixture is homogenous.
3. Add salt, thyme, and avocado oil and knead the soft dough.
4. Leave it for 10 minutes in a warm place.
5. After this, make a log from the dough and cut it into 12 pieces.
6. Roll up the dough pieces in the shape of rounds and put them in the hot skillet.
7. Cook every pita for 2-3 minutes from each side.

Per serving: 99 calories, 2.9g protein, 14.6g carbohydrates, 3.9g fat, 2.5g fiber, 0mg cholesterol, 52mg sodium, 88mg potassium.

Hummus Bread

Yield: 1 serving | **Prep time:** 7 minutes
Cook time: 0 minutes

Ingredients:

- 1 naan bread, toasted
- 1 teaspoon hummus
- ½ red onion, chopped
- ½ tomato, chopped
- 2 olives, pitted, chopped

Directions:

1. Spread the naan bread with hummus and top with onion, tomato, and olives.

Per serving: 97 calories, 3.6g protein, 17.5g carbohydrates, 1.8g fat, 1.7g fiber, 0mg cholesterol, 14mg sodium, 306mg potassium.

Parmesan Bites

Yield: 4 serving | **Prep time:** 7 minutes
Cook time: 10 minutes

Ingredients:

- 4 sandwich pepperoni slices
- 2 oz Parmesan, shaved
- 1 tablespoon pizza sauce

Directions:

1. Arrange the pepperoni slices in the muffin molds (in the shape of the cups).
2. Bake the pepperoni slices for 5 minutes at 400F.
3. Then add pizza sauce and shaved Parmesan in every pepperoni cup.
4. Cook the pizza bites for 5 minutes at 400F more.

Per serving: 173 calories, 9.1g protein, 2g carbohydrates, 13.6g fat, 0.1g fiber, 38mg cholesterol, 641mg sodium, 2mg potassium.

DESSERTS

Desserts

Vanilla Pears

Yield: 2 servings | **Prep time:** 10 minutes
Cook time: 20 minutes

Ingredients:

- 2 pears
- 1 teaspoon vanilla extract
- 1 teaspoon liquid honey

Directions:

1. Cut the peats into wedges and put them in the casserole mold in one layer.
2. Sprinkle the fruits with vanilla extract.
3. Bake the pears at 365F for 20 minutes.
4. Top the cooked pears with liquid honey.

per serving: 183 calories, 0.9g protein, 35g carbohydrates, 6.1g fat, 7.1g fiber, 15mg cholesterol, 44mg sodium, 256mg potassium.

Pecan Tart

Yield: 6 servings | **Prep time:** 15 minutes
Cook time: 30 minutes

Ingredients:

- 5 oz puff pastry
- 1 egg, beaten
- 4 pecans, chopped

Directions:

1. Roll up the puff pastry and transfer it to the square baking pan.
2. Sprinkle the puff pastry with pecans.
3. Then sprinkle it with egg and bake at 375F for 30 minutes or until the tart is light brown.

per serving: 156 calories, 3g protein, 11.2g carbohydrates, 11.3g fat, 0.6g fiber, 35mg cholesterol, 61mg sodium, 39mg potassium.

Raspberry Compote

Yield: 6 servings | **Prep time:** 15 minutes
Cook time: 14 minutes

Ingredients:

- 3 cups raspberries
- ½ cup cherries, raw
- 1 tablespoon fresh basil
- 3 cups of water

Directions:

1. Mix raspberries, cherries, fresh basil, and water in the saucepan.
2. Bring the mixture to a boil and remove from heat.
3. Cool the compote and serve it with ice cubes.

per serving: 31 calories, 0.7g protein, 7. g 4carbohydrates, 0.3g fat, 1.8g fiber, 0mg cholesterol, 5mg sodium, 141mg potassium

Sweet Almonds

Yield: 3 servings | **Prep time:** 10 minutes
Cook time: 2 minutes

Ingredients:

- 1 tablespoon liquid honey
- 2 oz almonds, chopped
- 1 teaspoon ground cinnamon

Directions:

1. Mix ingredients in the ramekin and microwave for 2 minutes.
2. Carefully whisk the mixture and cool.

per serving: 126 calories, 4.9g protein, 8.1g carbohydrates, 9.3g fat, 2g fiber, 0mg cholesterol, 4mg sodium, 150mg potassium.

Avocado Ice Cream

Yield: 4 servings | **Prep time:** 8 minutes
Cook time: 15 minutes

Ingredients:

- 2 avocadoes, peeled, chopped, and frozen
- 2 cups Greek yogurt
- ½ teaspoon vanilla extract
- 1 tablespoon liquid honey

Directions:

1. Put avocadoes in the food processor.
2. Add greek yogurt, liquid honey, and vanilla extract and blend the mixture until smooth.
3. Pour the cooked ice cream into the ramekins and freeze for 15 minutes in the freezer.

per serving: 130 calories, 10.7g protein, 17.6g carbohydrates, 2.2g fat, 1.5g fiber, 5mg cholesterol, 33mg sodium, 353mg potassium.

Papaya Sorbet

Yield: 2 servings | **Prep time:** 7 minutes
Cook time: 20 minutes

Ingredients:

- 1 papaya, pitted, peeled
- ¼ cup of water
- 1 tablespoon apple juice

Directions:

1. Chop papaya and blend it until you get a smooth puree.

2. After this, mix papaya puree with water and apple juice.
3. Transfer the papaya mixture to ramekins and freeze for 20 minutes.
4. Then churn the cooked sorbet.

per serving: 104 calories, 1.4g protein, 26g carbohydrates, 0.7g fat, 2.7g fiber, 0mg cholesterol, 3mg sodium, 298mg potassium.

Apricot Pie

Yield: 8 servings | Prep time: 15 minutes
Cook time: 40 minutes

Ingredients:

- 1 cup apricot, pitted, chopped
- ½ teaspoon ground cinnamon
- 1 egg, beaten
- 6 oz puff pastry

Directions:

1. Roll up the puff pastry and put it in the round baking pan.
2. Then add apricots.
3. Sprinkle the apricots with cinnamon and brush with beaten egg.
4. Bake the apricot pie for 40 minutes at 365F.

per serving: 146 calories, 2.5g protein, 11.5g carbohydrates, 10.2g fat, 0.6g fiber, 24mg cholesterol, 71mg sodium, 58mg potassium.

Chia Seeds Bars

Yield: 6 servings | Prep time: 15 minutes
Cook time: 8 minutes

Ingredients:

- ½ cup puffed quinoa
- 3 oz chia seeds, chopped
- 1 tablespoon vanilla extract
- 3 tablespoons liquid honey
- 1 tablespoon coconut shred

Directions:

1. Line the baking tray with baking paper.
2. Then mix all ingredients in the bowl.
3. Transfer the chia seeds mixture to the tray and flatten it.
4. Cut the flat mixture into bars with the help of the knife and bake at 360F for 8 minutes.
5. Cool the cooked bars well.

per serving: 141 calories, 3.9g protein, 14.3g carbohydrates, 7.8g fat, 1.6g fiber, 0mg cholesterol, 40mg sodium, 115mg potassium.

Stuffed Apricots

Yield: 4 servings | Prep time: 10 minutes
Cook time: 17 minutes

Ingredients:

- 4 apricots, halved, pitted
- 3 oz Feta cheese, crumbled
- 1 tablespoon liquid honey
- 1 teaspoon ground nutmeg

Directions:

1. Put the apricot halves in the tray.
2. Fill every apricot with crumbled Feta and sprinkle with ground nutmeg.
3. Bake the apricots at 365F for 17 minutes.
4. Sprinkle the cooked fruits with liquid honey.

per serving: 151 calories, 6.1g protein, 19.9g carbohydrates, 6.6g fat, 3.1g fiber, 20mg cholesterol, 266mg sodium, 290mg potassium.

Blackberry Parfait

Yield: 2 servings | Prep time: 10 minutes
Cook time: 0 minutes

Ingredients:

- ½ cup blackberries
- ¼ cup plain yogurt
- 1 tablespoon almond flakes

Directions:

1. Mix up together Plain yogurt and almond flakes.
2. Then put ½ part of all blackberries in the serving glasses.
3. Top the berries with ½ part of the yogurt.
4. Then add the remaining blackberries and yogurt.

per serving: 63 calories, 2.1g protein, 6.8g carbohydrates, 3.1g fat, 2.5g fiber, 2mg cholesterol, 23mg sodium, 118mg potassium.

Raspberry Muffins

Yield: 4 servings | Prep time: 15 minutes
Cook time: 12 minutes

Ingredients:

- 1/2 cup whole-grain wheat flour
- ½ ground oatmeal
- 1 teaspoon baking powder
- 3 oz raspberries
- 1 tablespoon avocado oil
- ¼ cup of water
- Cooking spray

Directions:

1. Mix whole-grain flour and oatmeal.

2. Add baking powder and avocado oil.
3. Then add water and stir the mixture until you get a smooth batter.
4. Add raspberries and stir the batter with the help of the spatula.
5. Fill ½ part of every muffin mold and bake them for 12 minutes at 375F.

per serving: 115 calories, 2.4g protein, 18g carbohydrates, 4.5g fat, 2.5g fiber, 1mg cholesterol, 23mg sodium, 203mg potassium.

Baked Pears

Yield: 4 servings | **Prep time:** 10 minutes
Cook time: 16 minutes

Ingredients:

- 4 pears, halved
- 1 tablespoon brown sugar
- ½ tablespoon ground cinnamon

Directions:

1. Line the baking tray with baking paper.
2. Then put the pears in the tray and flatten them in one layer.
3. Sprinkle the pears with brown sugar and ground cinnamon.
4. Bake them for 15 minutes at 365F.

per serving: 68 calories, 1g protein, 16.7g carbohydrates, 0.3g fat, 1.6g fiber, 0mg cholesterol, 2mg sodium, 184mg potassium.

Figs Pie

Yield: 6 servings | **Prep time:** 15 minutes
Cook time: 30 minutes

Ingredients:

- 6 oz puff pastry
- 4 oz figs, chopped
- 1 teaspoon vanilla extract
- 1 teaspoon almond butter, melted

Directions:

1. Roll up the puff pastry and put it in the pie mold.
2. Then brush the puff pastry pie crust with almond butter and top with chopped figs.
3. Sprinkle the figs with vanilla extract and bake at 360F for 30 minutes.
4. Cool the pie well and cut it into servings.

per serving: 227 calories, 3.1g protein, 27.8g carbohydrates, 12.4g fat, 2.4g fiber, 0mg cholesterol, 71mg sodium, 163mg potassium.

Lime Muffins

Yield: 12 servings | **Prep time:** 10 minutes
Cook time: 14 minutes

Ingredients:

- 3 eggs, beaten
- ¼ cup coconut milk
- 2 cups whole-grain flour
- 1 teaspoon vanilla extract
- 1 tablespoon lime zest, grated
- 2 tablespoons of liquid honey
- 3 tablespoons lime juice
- 1 teaspoon baking powder

Directions:

1. Mix all ingredients in the mixing bowl and blend with the help of the immersion blender until smooth.
2. Pour the batter into the muffin molds (fill ½ part of every muffin mold).
3. Bake the muffins for 14 minutes at 355F.

per serving: 97 calories, 4.2g protein, 18g carbohydrates, 1.5g fat, 2.5g fiber, 41mg cholesterol, 20mg sodium, 143mg potassium.

Almond Biscuits

Yield: 6 servings | **Prep time:** 15 minutes
Cook time: 8 minutes

Ingredients:

- 1 cup almond flakes
- 3 egg whites
- 1 teaspoon vanilla extract

Directions:

1. Whisk the egg whites gently and combine them with almond flakes and vanilla extract.
2. Make the small balls from the almond mixture and put them in the tray.
3. Bake the almond biscuits for 8 minutes at 365F.

per serving: 107 calories, 2.7g protein, 5.8g carbohydrates, 8.9g fat, 1.8g fiber, 0mg cholesterol, 21mg sodium, 28mg potassium.

Pecan Pie

Yield: 6 servings | **Prep time:** 20 minutes
Cook time: 15 minutes

Ingredients:

- 6 pecans, chopped
- ½ cup coconut flour
- 1 teaspoon vanilla extract
- ¼ teaspoon baking powder
- 2 tablespoons whole-grain flour

- 1 tablespoon liquid honey

Directions:

1. Mix coconut flour, vanilla extract, baking powder, honey, and whole-grain flour in the food processor. Knead the soft, non-sticky dough.
2. After this, put the dough in the round baking pan and flatten it into the shape of the pie crust with the help of your fingertips.
3. Sprinkle the pie crust with pecans.
4. Bake the pie for 15 minutes at 365F or until the edges of the pie are light brown.

per serving: 172 calories, 3.3g protein, 12.7g carbohydrates, 12.9g fat, 1.8g fiber, 10mg cholesterol, 35mg sodium, 35mg potassium.

Strawberry Tart

Yield: 6 servings | **Prep time:** 15 minutes
Cook time: 25 minutes

Ingredients:

- 1 cup strawberries
- 1 cup coconut flour
- 4 tablespoons olive oil
- ½ teaspoon baking powder
- 1 tablespoon liquid honey
- 1 teaspoon vanilla extract

Directions:

1. Mix coconut flour, baking powder, vanilla extract, and oil. Knead the soft dough.
2. Then put the dough in the tart pan and flatten it into the shape of the pie crust.
3. Put the strawberries over the pie crust in one layer and bake at 375F for 25 minutes.
4. Cool the tart to room temperature and sprinkle with liquid honey.

per serving: 216 calories, 4.3g protein, 9.6g carbohydrates, 18.3g fat, 3.4g fiber, 0mg cholesterol, 7mg sodium, 76mg potassium.

Vanilla Cookies

Yield: 10 servings | **Prep time:** 20 minutes
Cook time: 10 minutes

Ingredients:

- 2 tablespoons olive oil
- 1 teaspoon vanilla extract
- 2 oz coconut flour
- 2 eggs, beaten
- ½ teaspoon baking powder
- ½ teaspoon lemon juice
- 1 cup flour, whole grain

Directions:

1. Put all ingredients in the food processor.
2. Knead the smooth dough.
3. After this, cut the dough into 10 pieces and roll the balls
4. Then press every ball in the small cookie.
5. Line the baking tray with baking paper and put the prepared cookies inside.
6. Bake the cookies at 365F for 10 minutes.

per serving: 113 calories, 2.8g protein, 13.2g carbohydrates, 5.4g fat, 0.5g fiber, 34mg cholesterol, 17mg sodium, 72mg potassium.

Walnut Cookies

Yield: 6 servings | **Prep time:** 20 minutes
Cook time: 14 minutes

Ingredients:

- 7 oz all-purpose flour
- ½ cup walnuts, chopped
- 1 tablespoon cocoa powder
- 1 tablespoon Erythritol
- 1 teaspoon vanilla extract
- 2 eggs, beaten
- ¼ cup coconut milk

Directions:

1. Mix all-purpose flour, cocoa powder, Erythritol, and eggs.
2. Then add coconut milk and walnuts. Knead the dough.
3. Roll up the dough and make the cookies with the help of the cutter.
4. Place the cookies in the tray and bake at 365F for 14 minutes or until they are light brown.

per serving: 213 calories, 6.5g protein, 30.1g carbohydrates, 8.7g fat, 2.2g fiber, 55mg cholesterol, 27mg sodium, 117mg potassium.

Vanilla Tiramisu

Yield: 6 servings | **Prep time:** 35 minutes
Cook time: 0 minutes

Ingredients:

- 5 oz ladyfingers cookies
- ½ cup coconut milk
- 1 tablespoon coconut shred
- 1 cup cream cheese
- 1 teaspoon vanilla extract

Directions:

1. Mix cream cheese with vanilla extract.
2. Dip every ladyfinger cookie in the coconut milk.
3. Then make the layer from the cookies in the casserole

mold.

4. Top it with cream cheese.
5. Repeat the steps till you use all ingredients.
6. Then sprinkle the last layer (cream layer) with coconut shred.
7. Leave the cooked tiramisu in the fridge for 15 minutes before serving.

per serving: 149 calories, 3.1g protein, 15.3g carbohydrates, 8.5g fat, 0.5g fiber, 74mg cholesterol, 42mg sodium, 79mg potassium.

Raspberries Mousse

Yield: 2 servings | **Prep time:** 15 minutes
Cook time: 0 minutes

Ingredients:

- 1 cup cream cheese
- ½ cup raspberries
- 1 teaspoon almond flakes

Directions:

1. Blend cream cheese and raspberries.
2. Transfer the cooked mousse to the serving glasses and top with almond flakes.

per serving: 97 calories, 1.2g protein, 6.9g carbohydrates, 7.6g fat, 0.9g fiber, 23mg cholesterol, 40mg sodium, 99mg potassium.

Quinoa Crumble

Yield: 2 servings | **Prep time:** 15 minutes
Cook time: 25 minutes

Ingredients:

- ½ cup quinoa, cooked
- 2 bananas, chopped
- ¼ cup cream cheese
- 2 tablespoons almond flakes
- ¼ teaspoon ground cinnamon

Directions:

1. Mix ground cinnamon with almond flakes and cream cheese.
2. Then separate the cream cheese mixture into 3 parts.
3. Put the first cream cheese mixture in the glasses.
4. Top them with quinoa, and add cream cheese again.
5. After this, add bananas, and the remaining cream cheese.
6. Leave the crumbled for 25 minutes in the fridge.

per serving: 277 calories, 4.3g protein, 43.5g carbohydrates, 11.4g fat, 6.3g fiber, 17mg cholesterol, 10mg sodium, 512mg potassium.

Chia Pudding

Yield: 4 servings | **Prep time:** 15 minutes
Cook time: 0 minutes

Ingredients:

- 1 teaspoon vanilla extract
- 4 oz chia seeds
- 2 cups coconut milk
- 1 tablespoon liquid honey
- 1 pecan, chopped

Directions:

1. Pour coconut milk into the saucepan and bring to a boil. Remove it from the heat.
2. Add chia seeds and vanilla extract. Stir the ingredients with the help of a spoon.
3. Stir the chia pudding and leave for 10 minutes.
4. Then put the cooked pudding in the bowl and sprinkle it with pecans and honey.

per serving: 227 calories, 3.9g protein, 43.9g carbohydrates, 3.4g fat, 1g fiber, 0mg cholesterol, 38mg sodium, 72mg potassium.

Meringue Clouds

Yield: 8 servings | **Prep time:** 15 minutes
Cook time: 120 minutes

Ingredients:

- 3 egg whites
- 1 cup Erythritol
- 1 teaspoon vanilla extract
- 1 teaspoon lemon juice

Directions:

1. Preheat the oven to 295F.
2. Then whisk the egg whites until firm peaks.
3. Add Erythritol, vanilla extract, and lemon juice, and whisk the egg whites until stiff peaks.
4. Line the baking tray with baking paper.
5. Then make the small clouds with the help of the spoon and put them in the tray.
6. Bake the dessert for 120 minutes.

per serving: 6 calories, 1.4g protein, 30.1g carbohydrates, 0g fat, 0g fiber, 0mg cholesterol, 12mg sodium, 20mg potassium.

Banana Panna Cotta

Yield: 2 servings | **Prep time:** 45 minutes
Cook time: 8 minutes

Ingredients:

- ½ cup coconut milk
- 2 bananas, peeled, mashed
- 1 tablespoon gelatin

- 3 tablespoons apple juice

Directions:

1. Mix apple juice and gelatin and leave for 10 minutes.
2. Then preheat the coconut milk until warm and add gelatin. Stir the liquid until the gelatin is dissolved.
3. Then pour ½ part of the liquid into the glasses and freeze until solid.
4. Add mashed banana and the remaining cream.
5. Refrigerate the panna cotta for 30 minutes in the fridge.

per serving: 6 calories, 3.8g protein, 10.8g carbohydrates, 0.8g fat, 0.7g fiber, 0mg cholesterol, 42mg sodium, 118mg potassium.

Stuffed Pears

Yield: 5 servings | **Prep time:** 15 minutes
Cook time: 25 minutes

Ingredients:

- 5 pears
- 5 teaspoons raisins, chopped
- 1 tablespoon walnuts, chopped
- 1 teaspoon raspberry puree

Directions:

1. Core the pears.
2. Then mix the raspberry puree with raisins and walnuts.
3. Fill the cored pears with a raisin mixture and transfer them to the oven.
4. Bake the pears for 25 minutes at 375F.
5. Cool the cooked pears to room temperature.

per serving: 140 calories, 0.7g protein, 34.9g carbohydrates, 1.4g fat, 5.7g fiber, 0mg cholesterol, 3mg sodium, 261mg potassium.

Pancake Pie

Yield: 6 servings | **Prep time:** 15 minutes
Cook time: 15 minutes

Ingredients:

- 1 teaspoon baking powder
- 3 eggs, beaten
- ½ cup flour, whole-grain
- 6 oz sour cream
- 1 oz almonds, chopped
- 1 tablespoon liquid honey
- 1 tablespoon olive oil

Directions:

1. Make the pancakes: mix baking powder, eggs, flour, and olive oil. Whisk the mixture until smooth.

2. Then preheat the non-stick skillet.
3. Make the pancakes. Cook them for 1.5 minutes per side.
4. Then churn sour cream with liquid honey and almonds.
5. Spread every pancake with the sour cream mixture and combine them in the shape of a pie.

per serving: 229 calories, 7.1g protein, 12.6g carbohydrates, 17.3g fat, 0.6g fiber, 113mg cholesterol, 116mg sodium, 185mg potassium.

Banana Shake

Yield: 3 servings | **Prep time:** 10 minutes
Cook time: 0 minutes

Ingredients:

- 1 banana, peeled and chopped
- 1 tablespoon cream cheese
- 1 cup coconut milk
- 1 teaspoon vanilla extract

Directions:

1. Blend banana until smooth.
2. Add coconut milk, cream cheese, and vanilla extract.
3. Pulse the shake for 10 seconds and pour in the glasses.

per serving: 127 calories, 1.4g protein, 14.7g carbohydrates, 7.5g fat, 3.3g fiber, 0mg cholesterol, 4mg sodium, 305g potassium.

Cinnamon Pudding

Yield: 4 servings | **Prep time:** 15 minutes
Cook time: 10 minutes

Ingredients:

- 2 tablespoons Erythritol
- 2 cups coconut milk
- 1 tablespoon flour
- 4 egg yolks, whisked
- 1 teaspoon ground cinnamon

Directions:

1. Whisk coconut milk with egg yolks, ground cinnamon, flour, and Erythritol.
2. Simmer the mixture for 10 minutes on low heat. Stir the pudding constantly.
3. Then cool the cooked dessert.

per serving: 94 calories, 3.4g protein, 13.7g carbohydrates, 5.8g fat, 0.1g fiber, 210mg cholesterol, 78mg sodium, 22mg potassium.

Cocoa Glass

Yield: 1 serving | **Prep time:** 10 minutes
Cook time: 0 minutes

Ingredients:

- 1 tablespoon cocoa powder
- 5 tablespoons sour cream
- 2 strawberries

Directions:

1. Mash the strawberries and put them in the bottom of the glass.
2. Then whisk cocoa powder with sour cream and top the strawberries.

per serving: 86 calories, 5.8g protein, 12.9g carbohydrates, 1.9g fat, 4.1g fiber, 5mg cholesterol, 55mg sodium, 372mg potassium.

Vanilla Nectarines

Yield: 2 servings | **Prep time:** 10 minutes
Cook time: 15 minutes

Ingredients:

- 2 nectarines, halved, pitted
- 1 teaspoon vanilla extract
- 2 teaspoons honey

Directions:

1. In the shallow bowl mix honey and vanilla extract. Churn the mixture.
2. Then fill every nectarine half with the honey mixture and bake at 365F for 15 minutes.

per serving: 138 calories, 1.6g protein, 21.7g carbohydrates, 6.2g fat, 3g fiber, 15mg cholesterol, 41mg sodium, 296mg potassium.

Lemon Fudge

Yield: 4 servings | **Prep time:** 20 minutes
Cook time: 0 minutes

Ingredients:

- 1/3 cup almond butter
- 1 tablespoon olive oil
- 2 tablespoons lemon juice
- 1 teaspoon lemon zest
- 1 tablespoon Erythritol

Directions:

1. Mix almond butter and olive oil.
2. Add lemon juice, lemon zest, and Erythritol.
3. Churn the mixture until it is soft and fluffy.
4. Then line the baking tray with baking paper.
5. Spread the fudge mixture over the baking paper and flatten well.

6. Freeze it until solid.
7. Then cut the fudge into serving bars.

per serving: 41 calories, 0.3g protein, 4.6g carbohydrates, 4.3g fat, 0.2g fiber, 0mg cholesterol, 1mg sodium, 17mg potassium.

Millet Mousse

Yield: 4 servings | **Prep time:** 10 minutes
Cook time: 10 minutes

Ingredients:

- 4 oz millet
- 1 cup coconut milk
- 1 teaspoon vanilla extract
- ¼ cup mango puree

Directions:

1. Bring the coconut milk to a boil, and add millet.
2. Simmer it for 5 minutes and add vanilla extract, and mango puree. Bring the mousse to a boil and remove it from the heat.
3. Cool the cooked meal to room temperature, and transfer it to the serving ramekins.

per serving: 126 calories, 3.9g protein, 24.3g carbohydrates, 1g fat, 1.3g fiber, 0mg cholesterol, 35mg sodium, 72mg potassium.

Grilled Pineapple

Yield: 3 servings | **Prep time:** 7 minutes
Cook time: 2 minutes

Ingredients:

- 10 oz pineapple, peeled, roughly chopped
- 1 tablespoon Erythritol
- ¼ teaspoon ground nutmeg

Directions:

1. Then mix Erythritol and ground nutmeg.
2. Sprinkle the pineapple with the ground nutmeg mixture and grill in the preheated to 375F grill for 1 minute per side.

per serving: 141 calories, 1.4g protein, 27.2g carbohydrates, 4.3g fat, 3.1g fiber, 10mg cholesterol, 29mg sodium, 431mg potassium.

Mango Pie

Yield: 6 servings | **Prep time:** 15 minutes
Cook time: 40 minutes

Ingredients:

- 1 cup mango, chopped
- 1 cup whole-grain flour
- 1 teaspoon baking powder
- 1 tablespoon lemon juice

- 5 eggs, beaten

Directions:

1. Whisk eggs with baking powder, lemon juice, and flour.
2. When you get a smooth batter, add mango and stir.
3. Then pour the batter into the non-stick baking pan, flatten, and transfer it to the oven.
4. Bake the pie for 40 minutes at 365F.
5. Cool the pie and cut it into servings.

per serving: 135 calories, 7.5g protein, 18.8g carbohydrates, 4g fat, 2.8g fiber, 136mg cholesterol, 54mg sodium, 246mg potassium.

60-Day Meal Plan

DAY	BREAKFAST	LUNCH	SNACK	DINNER
1	Quinoa Bowl Chickpea Salad	Chicken Breast and Pepper Skillet Coriander Chicken	Faro Skillet	Tomato Beans Vanilla Pears Meat and Garbanzo Beans
2	Cinnamon Pancakes Cheddar Cheese Salad Cheddar Chicken	Millet Mousse	Baked Mackerel with Goat Cheese	Bean Wrap Sweet Almonds Sweet Potato Soup
3	Artichoke Eggs Raisins Salad	Italian Style Chicken Strawberry Tart	Seared Halibut Red Salad	Lettuce and Beans Bowl Avocado Ice Cream
4	Cod Eggs Pesto Sauce Salad	Basil Chicken Cheddar Pizza	Thyme Swordfish Quinoa Crumble	Oregano Beans Papaya Sorbet Garlic Zucchini
5	Lentil Bowl Goat Cheese Pizza	Chicken Kebab Bean Mix	Stuffed Tilapia	White Beans Bowl Apricot Pie
6	Onion Beans Beef Salad Cheddar Spread	Honey Chicken Wings Quinoa Bowl	Chicken and Parsley Rice Banana Salad	Tender Garlic Dip Pecan Tart
7	Quinoa with Pecans Greece Style Salad	Jalapeno Chicken Thighs Lentil Bowl	Walnut Oats	Beans and Tomatoes Ragout Chia Seeds Bars
8	Mozzarella Bowl Goat Cheese Salad	Chicken and Pepper Tray Green Beans Soup	Dill Mashed Potato Seabass Puttanesca	Meat and Garbanzo Beans Stuffed Apricots Kale Rolls
9	Eggs with Tender Chicken Yogurt Salad	Lime Chicken Bean Pate	Pancake Pie Cheese Tortillas	Beans and Meat Stew Raspberry Muffins
10	Beans and Seeds Salad Prune Salad	Nutmeg Chicken Drumsticks Cauliflower Soup	Onion Salad	Garlic Beans Almond Biscuits
11	Fish Muffins Almond Salad with Fennel	Coriander Chicken Sweet Potato Soup	Figs Pie	Beans and Seafood Salad Pecan Pie Vegetable Pilaf
12	Feta Frittata Quinoa Salad with Artichoke	Za'atar Chicken Breast Vanilla Tiramisu	Bean Wrap	Simple Meat and Beans Soup Strawberry Tart Mint and Chicken Pilaf
13	Salmon Sandwich Feta and Herbs Salad	Cumin Beef Bites Parmesan Bites	Lime Chicken Onion Beans	Bean Pate Vanilla Cookies
14	Oat Muffins Onion Salad	Thyme Beef Steak Banana Shake	Cinnamon Butternut Squash Bean Wrap	Lunch Bean Spread Walnut Cookies
15	Dill Eggs Orange Salad	Beef Casserole Green Beans Soup	Eggplant and Rice	Cannellini Beans and Cucumber Mix Figs Pie Banana Salad
16	Walnut Oats Red Salad	Plain Pork Steak Turmeric Zucchini Rounds	Salmon in Lemon Marinade	Bean Mix Vanilla Tiramisu Cannellini Beans Soup

DAY	BREAKFAST	LUNCH	SNACK	DINNER
17	Sweet Paprika Eggs Tilapia Salad	Clove Pork Loin Lentil Bowl	Garlic Pizza	Greek-Style Baked Beans Chia Pudding Chicken and Parsley Rice
18	Shiitake Mushrooms Casserole Easy Caesar	Tender Beef and Tomatoes Stew Green Beans Soup	Garlic Zucchini	Bean and Mozzarella Dip Quinoa Crumble Tomatoes Rice
19	Cinnamon Pancakes Blackberry Eggs	Pork Medallions in Yogurt Gravy Lentil Bowl	Chicken Flatbread Russet Potato Frittata	Grilled Cod with Edamame Beans Stuffed Pears Pecan Dates
20	Chives Galettes Pomegranate Salad	Rosemary Lamb Chops Chicken Chowder	Parmesan Bites Quinoa with Pecans	Winter Beans Stew Pancake Pie
21	Artichoke Eggs Banana Salad	Salmon Tacos	Spinach Pizza Quinoa with Pecans	Coriander Black Beans Banana Shake
22	Cheese Tortillas Garlic and Eggplants Salad	Coriander Seabass Feta Dip	Sprout Pizza Walnut Cookies	Beans and Pepper Vanilla Nectarines Beef Casserole
23	Lentil Bowl Heart of Palm and Feta Salad	Cumin Shrimps Pecan Pie	Goat Cheese Pizza Pancake Pie	Green Beans Soup Millet Mousse
24	Strawberry Bars Spinach Mix	Salmon Coated in Cheese	Strawberry Tart Cheddar Pizza Lunch Bean Spread	Salmon Pie Grilled Pineapple Quinoa and Scallions Balls
25	Goat Cheese Sandwich Garlic Zucchini	Salmon in Lemon Marinade Cheddar Cheese Salad	Arugula Pizza Cinnamon Butternut Squash	Seared Halibut Mango Pie Pesto Sauce Salad
26	Mozzarella Bowl Grilled Ruby Chard	Yogurt Cod Pecan Pie	Dates Pizza Seared Halibut	Italian Style Chicken Vanilla Pears Butter Snap Peas
27	Onion Beans Thyme Baked Potatoes	Stuffed Tilapia Prune Salad	Tomato Tart Curry Brown Rice	Jalapeno Chicken Thighs Apricot Pie
28	Orange Salad Cinnamon Butternut Squash	Sheet-Pan Tilapia Figs Pie	Ricotta Cheese Pizza Italian Style Rice	Lime Chicken Pecan Tart Beef Soup
29	Russet Potato Frittata Parsley Mushrooms	Pepper Fish Tender Garlic Dip	Olives Pizza Lentil Bowl	Coriander Chicken Chia Seeds Bars
30	Apple Quinoa Seasoned Chickpeas	Stuffed Halibut	Blackberry Eggs Parmesan Bites Salmon Coated in Cheese	Winter Beans Stew Chia Pudding
31	Eggs with Tender Chicken Provolone Cheese Asparagus	Baked Mackerel with Goat Cheese	Sheet-Pan Tilapia Sprout Pizza	Thyme Beef Steak Quinoa Crumble
32	Beans and Seeds Salad Almonds and Greens Bowl	Za'atar Mackerel	Seared Halibut Parmesan Bites Beef Casserole	Beef Casserole Stuffed Apricots Plain Pork Steak
33	Salmon Sandwich Garlic and Hazelnuts Beets	Salmon Pie Cheesy Buckwheat	Chicken Pizza Rosemary Lamb Chops	Pecan Pie

DAY	BREAKFAST	LUNCH	SNACK	DINNER
34	Oat Muffins	Thyme Swordfish	Sprout Pizza	Clove Pork Loin
	Turmeric Zucchini Rounds	Strawberry Tart	Onion Soup	Strawberry Tart
35	Quinoa Bowl	Seared Halibut	Chicken Pizza	Tender Beef and Tomatoes Stew
	Thyme Sweet Potato		Plain Pork Steak	Walnut Cookies
36	Chives Galettes	Tilapia Tapas	Tomato Tart	Rosemary Lamb Chops
	Feta and Dill Beets		Pancake Pie	Vanilla Pears
			Za'atar Mackerel	Cheddar Cheese Salad
37	Artichoke Eggs	Chicken Breast and Pepper Skillet	Olives Antipasti	Salmon Coated in Cheese
	Butter Snap Peas	Lentil Bowl	Rosemary Lamb Chops	Sweet Almonds
38	Quinoa with Pecans	Italian Style Chicken	Onion Salad	Stuffed Tilapia
	Dill Mashed Potato	Mercimek Soup	Beans and Seafood Salad	Avocado Ice Cream
39	Onion Salad	Basil Chicken	Garlic Baby Potatoes	Sheet-Pan Tilapia
	Fast Tomatoes Salad	Chicken Chowder	Rice with Apricots	Papaya Sorbet
				Garlic and Hazelnuts Beets
40	Rice with Apricots	Jalapeno Chicken Thighs	Kale Rolls	Stuffed Halibut
	Cucumbers and Bocconcini Bowl	Cannellini Beans Soup		Apricot Pie
41	Tender Quinoa	Lime Chicken	Greece Style Chickpeas	Baked Mackerel with Goat Cheese
	Paprika Avocado Bites	Red Kidney Beans Soup	Green Beans Soup	Pecan Tart
42	Tomatoes Rice	Coriander Chicken	Cheesy Buckwheat	Thyme Swordfish
	Chicken Pizza	Pepper Soup	Red Salad	Chia Seeds Bars
				Ginger Salad with Yogurt
43	Vegetable Pilaf	Thyme Beef Steak	Beans and Meat Stew	Seared Halibut
	Beef Pizza	Onion Soup	Feta Dip	Stuffed Apricots
44	Chicken and Parsley Rice	Beef Casserole	Eggs with Tender Chicken	Tomato Beans
	Fluffy Bread with Olives	Cucumber Soup	Banana Salad	Raspberry Muffins
45	Chives and Jasmine Rice	Plain Pork Steak	Olives Antipasti	Bean Wrap
	Chicken Flatbread	Rice with Apricots	Tender Basil Artichoke	Almond Biscuits
46	Celery Rice	Clove Pork Loin	Rice and Cheese Meatballs	Lettuce and Beans Bowl
	Parmesan Bites	Sweet Potato Soup	Beef Salad	Pecan Pie
47	Beef and Rice Bowl	Tender Beef and Tomatoes Stew	Chickpea Salad	Lime Chicken
	Spinach Pizza	Chicken Chowder		Strawberry Tart
48	Tomatoes Rice	Cumin Shrimps	Salmon Pie	Meat and Garbanzo Beans
	Sprout Pizza	Cannellini Beans Soup	Rice and Cheese Meatballs	Vanilla Cookies
49	Eggplant and Rice	Salmon Coated in Cheese	Chicken Flatbread	Beans and Meat Stew
	Goat Cheese Pizza		Thyme Baked Potatoes	Walnut Cookies
50	Rice Cakes	Salmon in Lemon Marinade		Bean Pate
	Cheddar Pizza	Cauliflower Soup		Figs Pie
51	Seafood and Rice Stew	Yogurt Cod	Chives and Jasmine Rice	Bean Mix
	Garlic Pizza	Red Kidney Beans Soup	Thyme Baked Potatoes	Vanilla Tiramisu
52	Salsa and Pesto Rice	Stuffed Tilapia	Feta Dip	Winter Beans Stew
	Tomato Tart	Cannellini Beans Soup	Vegetable Pilaf	Chia Pudding
53	Mint and Chicken Pilaf	Sheet-Pan Tilapia	Lettuce and Beans Bowl	Beans and Pepper
	Olives Pizza	Cucumber Soup		Quinoa Crumble

DAY	BREAKFAST	LUNCH	SNACK	DINNER
54	Cream Cheese Buckwheat	Pepper Fish	Red Salad	Green Beans Soup
	Parmesan Bites	Red Kidney Beans Soup	Salmon Coated in Cheese	Stuffed Pears
55	Cheesy Buckwheat	Stuffed Halibut	Green Beans Soup	Thyme Baked Potatoes
	Fluffy Bread with Olives	Pepper Soup		Pancake Pie
56	Pesto Millet	Baked Mackerel with Goat Cheese	Celery Stalk Soup	Almonds and Greens Bowl
	Feta and Dill Beets	Onion Soup	Lime Chicken	Banana Shake
57	Tender Quinoa	Salmon Pie	Seared Halibut	Thyme Sweet Potato
	Chickpea Salad	Chicken Chowder	Chili Lobster Tails	Vanilla Nectarines
58	Kale Rolls	Thyme Swordfish	Quinoa Salad with Artichoke	Feta and Dill Beets
	Pesto Sauce Salad	Cannellini Beans Soup	Quinoa Bowl	Millet Mousse
59	Honey Quinoa	Seared Halibut	Salmon Sandwich	Thyme Beef Steak
	Onion Salad		Bean Wrap	Grilled Pineapple
60	Feta Wild Rice	Tilapia Tapas	Baked Mackerel with Goat Cheese	Plain Pork Steak
	Cinnamon Butternut Squash	Cheesy Buckwheat		Mango Pie
				Lime Beans

RECIPE INDEX

Made in the USA
Monee, IL
11 April 2023